BOOK OF ISMS

OTHER ECONOMIST BOOKS

Guide to Analysing Companies
Guide to Business Modelling
Guide to Business Planning
Guide to Economic Indicators
Guide to the European Union
Guide to Financial Management
Guide to Financial Markets
Guide to Hedge Funds
Guide to Investment Strategy
Guide to Management Ideas and Gurus
Guide to Organisation Design
Guide to Project Management
Guide to Supply Chain Management
Numbers Guide
Style Guide

Book of Obituaries
Brands and Branding
Business Consulting
Buying Professional Services
The City
Coaching and Mentoring
Dealing with Financial Risk
Doing Business in China
Economics
Emerging Markets
The Future of Technology
Headhunters and How to Use Them
Mapping the Markets
Marketing
Organisation Culture
Successful Strategy Execution
The World of Business

Directors: an A–Z Guide
Economics: an A–Z Guide
Investment: an A–Z Guide
Negotiation: an A–Z Guide

Pocket World in Figures

Book of isms

from Abolitionism to Zoroastrianism

John Andrews

THE ECONOMIST IN ASSOCIATION WITH
PROFILE BOOKS LTD

Published by Profile Books Ltd
3A Exmouth House, Pine Street, London EC1R 0JH
www.profilebooks.com

Typeset in EcoType by MacGuru Ltd
info@macguru.org.uk

Printed and bound in Italy by
L.E.G.O. Spa Lavis (TN)

A CIP catalogue record for this book is available
from the British Library

ISBN 978 1 84668 298 8

To my son, Tom, a true wordsmith

Contents

Preface

What is an "ism"? The etymologists, harking back – via medieval French and Latin – to Greek words that end in "ismos", will say those three letters are a convenient suffix: add them to a noun or adjective, or to the stem of a verb, and, to the delight of philologists, you add meaning, distinction and nuance. Terror becomes terrorism; global becomes globalism; baptise becomes baptism. Inventive types will add "ism" to all manner of words – a "Bushism", for example, for any of the many malapropisms uttered by America's 43rd president. Bushism has the same linguistic form as Reaganism, or Thatcherism or Marxism, and yet is conceptually different. For Messrs Reagan, Thatcher and Marx, their "isms" define their political and economic ideologies; despite the existence of a Bush doctrine, his "ism" describes merely his verbal oddities.

Purists may argue that a list of isms should be confined to the doctrines of religion, the schools of philosophy, the vagaries of society or the mysteries of science and medicine. Our approach is more forgiving: Bushism enters our list because it means something just as clear, in its own way, as Marxism. So does schism, which is not properly speaking an "ism" at all (its last three letters are not a suffix but are part of the stem) but which is an informative little word given the number of religious "isms" that follow from one schism or another.

And because schism is in, prism must enter the list too – though it is surely intrinsically less interesting.

In the English language "isms" have existed since at least the late 17th century, and their number increases by the year. Dadaism could not exist before Dada – and Dada was not launched until 1916; Darwinism could not exist before Darwin. Most "isms" go hand-in-hand with an "ist": a Marxist believes in Marxism; a Calvinist in Calvinism. But the connection is by no means invariable: there is no "etymologism" for an etymologist, or "philologism" for the philologist. Yet because, thankfully, there is no English equivalent of the Académie française to determine what words are acceptable, there is nothing to stop anyone from inventing an "ism" and proffering it to the altars of either common usage or scholarly esoterica. Perhaps we shall soon be talking of "Facebookism".

But will our "isms" become "wasms", to paraphrase the judgment of the Hungarian-born American historian John Lukacs on the collapse of the Soviet Union (he made an exception for nationalism)? Let us hope not. "Isms" help to inform us, educate us and sometimes even amuse us. This collection of more than 400 is a modest attempt to keep them alive.

John Andrews
May 2010

a

Abolitionism A movement in Europe and the Americas
dedicated to ending slavery, including a transatlantic
slave trade that saw perhaps 15m Africans transported to
the Americas between the 15th and 19th centuries. The
British abolitionist movement was founded by Quakers
in 1873. Influenced by the campaigning zeal of William
Wilberforce (1759–1833), a British member of Parliament,
Britain outlawed the trading of slaves throughout its
empire in 1807 (the possession of slaves remained lawful
until 1834). France, which had originally condemned
slavery in its 1795 constitution, incorporating its
declaration of human rights, followed suit in 1848. In the
United States abolitionism can be traced to a Quaker
petition against slavery in 1688, but success was, to say
the least, gradual: northern states banned slavery in the
early 19th century, with the importation of slaves being
outlawed in 1808, but southern states considered slavery
an essential part of their economy and way of life
– hence the bloody American civil war of 1861–65. With
the defeat of the south and the subsequent passing of the
13th amendment of the Constitution, slavery was

formally ended in the United States in December 1865. In law, there is now no slavery in the world; in practice, the UN calculates that around 27m people worldwide live in slavery.

Absenteeism The state of being absent from the workplace – a frequent complaint by bosses, who may associate its rate in the workforce with trade-union membership. Boredom could be a reason, too.

Absolutism As a political doctrine, it asserts the unlimited authority and sovereignty of a central figure, for example a monarch unchecked by parliament, judges or clerics. As Louis XIV, the "sun king" who reigned in France from 1643 to 1715, famously put it, "*L'état, c'est moi*" (I am the state). The simple justification in the Europe of the 16th–18th centuries was "the divine right of kings", with the monarch deriving his authority from God. Modern tyrants also wield absolute power, but often claim to be exponents of democracy. As a philosophical concept, absolutism holds that certain values, such as truth, are unchanging. Relativists think otherwise (see relativism).

Abstract expressionism A school of non-figurative art that began in New York in the 1940s and 1950s, emphasising spontaneous creation – as in the "action" paintings of Jackson Pollock (1912–56), who would pour or drip paint onto a whole canvas. Other leading abstract expressionists (though their style differed from that of Pollock) were Mark Rothko (1903–70) and Dutch-born Willem de Kooning (1904–97). This New York school of painting, which in its origins was greatly influenced by Europeans, such as the painters Salvador Dali (1904–89) and Piet Mondrian (1872–1944) and the poet André Breton (1896–1966), in flight from the second world war, shifted the post-war centre of gravity of the art world from Europe to America.

Absurdism A philosophy, closely linked to existentialism and nihilism, that holds that mankind exists in a meaningless, irrational world, making absurd any search for order and meaning. Absurdism was intrinsic to the ideas of the 19th-century Danish philosopher Soran Kierkegaard (1813–55), but was popularised by the French-Algerian philosopher Albert Camus (1913–60) in his essay *The Myth of Sisyphus*. Much of modern theatre is influenced by absurdism: the idea that life is ultimately without purpose has attracted playwrights from Eugène Ionesco to Harold Pinter.

Aestheticism A European, and particularly British, cultural movement in the late 19th century that decreed that art exists for its beauty alone – *"L'art pour l'art"* (art for art's sake), as the French philosopher Victor Cousin (1792–1867) noted in 1818. The movement's origins can be traced back to the 18th century, with the German philosopher Immanuel Kant (1724–1804) arguing that aesthetic standards are separate from morality or utility. The artists of the British Pre-Raphaelite school, such as Edward Burne-Jones (1833–98) and Dante Gabriel Rossetti (1828–82), were prominent followers of the movement, reacting against the view of John Ruskin (1819–1900) and

William Morris (1834–96) that art must be connected to
morality.

Afrocentrism A view of the world that puts Africa, and by
extension any people of black African heritage, at the
centre. Afrocentrism was a concept developed mostly by
African-Americans, such as the scholar W.E.B. Du Bois
(1868–1963), in reaction to generations of western
oppression, either by colonialism or by slavery. The term
"Afrocentric" seems to have originated in 1961 or 1962,
possibly thanks to Du Bois, in a proposal for an
Encyclopedia Africana, which was to be "unashamedly
Afro-Centric but not indifferent to the impact of the
outside world". In 2000 the American scholar Molefi Kete
Asante (born Arthur Lee Smith Junior in 1942) gave a
lecture at Liverpool University in Britain entitled
"Afrocentricity: Toward a New Understanding of African
Thought in this Millennium". By the end of the 20th
century Afrocentrism had become a common theme in
Black Studies at many American universities.

Ageism Discrimination against the old on the basis of their
age. The word was coined in 1969 by an American
gerontologist, Robert Butler, and has since become an
essential part of any politically correct vocabulary, not
least because the voting power of the elderly in western
democracies has increased with greater life expectancy
and lower birth rates. In response, many governments
have passed laws forbidding compulsory retirement ages
and other such "ageist" measures. Culturally, ageism
seems embedded in the youth-admiring West, where

national leaders are often elected when they are in their 40s; by contrast, in East Asia old age commands respect, including in politics.

Agnosticism Strictly speaking the idea that man cannot know anything beyond his material experience, but – in common usage – the notion that man cannot prove or disprove the existence of God. The term "agnostic" (formed by prefixing the "privative alpha" to gnosis, the Greek word for knowledge) was first used in 1869 by the British biologist Thomas Huxley (1825–95) as a rejection of both traditional Judaeo-Christian theism and atheism. Atheists sometimes argue that agnostics simply lack the courage to deny the existence of God; agnostics counter that they are being intellectually honest.

Agrarianism A movement that holds that the cultivation of the soil – but not industrial farming – provides a happier, more satisfying life than societies based on the city and modern capitalism. Agrarian societies may have been the norm in the Middle Ages, but today they exist only in isolation: for example, the Amish and Mennonites in the United States, or hippy communes. Several European countries had agrarian parties in the early 20th century, but the only instance of an agrarian movement gaining political power was the tyrannical rule from 1975 to 1979 of Pol Pot's Khmers Rouges in Cambodia. For all the supposed attractions of agrarianism, the trend towards city-living seems ineluctable: according to the UN more than half of the world's population now live in urban areas, a milestone reached in 2008.

Alarmism The issuing of needless, or exaggerated warnings.
Opportunities for alarmists are legion: terrorism, disease
and natural disasters all invite pessimistic (see
pessimism), but ultimately inaccurate, predictions – for
example, the Y2K bug that was supposed to wreck
computer systems at the turn of the millennium, or the
risk that Saddam Hussein (c1937–2006) would unleash
weapons of mass destruction on the West. "Crying wolf"
is a common idiom for alarmism. However, alarmists are
not inevitably wrong: the curse of Cassandra, according
to Greek myth, was to make accurate prophecies that
were never believed.

Albigensianism A heretical Christian sect of Cathars (see
Catharism) that flourished in southern France in the 12th
and 13th centuries. The name comes from the town of
Albi, though the main centre of the Albigensians was in
Toulouse, to its south. The sect rejected the priestly
functions of the Roman Catholic church and believed in
a Manichaean dualism of spiritual good and material evil:
God and the evil one; light and dark. The Albigensians
admired extreme ascetism, including celibacy, and were
divided into two classes: the believers and the "perfect".
Those able to meet the sect's strict standards were the
perfect – and were, of course, a minority. The
Albigensians prospered in part because of their contrast
with a corrupt Catholic church, but in 1209 Pope
Innocent III launched a crusade against them, promising
that the land of the defeated Albigensians would pass to
his allies from northern France. The crusade lasted for 20
bloody years, ending with the destruction of Provençal

civilisation and passing control of the Languedoc region to the French monarchy. There then followed, under Pope Gregory IX, an investigation of the Albigensians by the Dominican order of monks – the beginning of the century-long Inquisition that crushed the movement forever.

Albinism The absence, by a congenital defect, of the melanin pigment in a person, leading skin to be white and eyes to be usually blue but occasionally red. The term, derived from the Latin *albus*, meaning white, originates in the early 18th century when the Portuguese noticed albinos among African blacks. The condition can also be found in birds and animals, though white tigers are not actually albinos.

Alcoholism An addiction, sometimes associated with mental illness, to alcoholic drinks, which an alcoholic consumes to excess. America's National Council on Alcoholism and Drug Dependence defines alcoholism as "a primary, chronic disease characterised by impaired control over drinking, preoccupation with the drug alcohol, use of alcohol despite adverse consequences, and distortions in thinking". The description of alcoholism as a disease, rather than simply a form of behaviour, became prevalent in the latter half of the 20th century and is not universally accepted. What is clear, however, is that alcoholics are disproportionately prone to health problems such as liver disease.

Altruism A doctrine – coined in the 19th century by the French philosopher Auguste Comte (1798–1857), the founder of positivism – that holds that individuals have a moral duty to seek the good of others. Altruism, the opposite of egoism and selfishness, is basic to many religions, from Christianity to Sikhism. One problem, however, is to define "the good", not least when short-term and long-term interests diverge or when the doer of good and the supposed beneficiary disagree.

American exceptionalism A notion, rooted in the admiring 19th-century commentary of the French historian Alexis de Tocqueville (1805–59), that the United States has a special place in the world as a nation of democracy, opportunity and immigrants. As the British writer G.K. Chesterton (1874–1936) noted, "America is the only nation in the world that is founded on a creed. That creed is set forth with dogmatic and even theological lucidity in the Declaration of Independence." The term, a favourite of political scientists after the second world war, has roots that are religious (as in the 17th-century metaphor that America "shall be a city upon a hill" and in the 19th-century theory of a conquering "manifest destiny"). But the roots are also social – America as a melting pot of races – and, indeed, environmental, given the variety of America's natural resources and geography. Unimpressed cynics note that many nations consider themselves exceptional, and critics argue that American exceptionalism is an excuse for jingoism and neo-imperialism.

Anabaptism The doctrine, held by radical Protestants, that baptism – signifying entry into the Christian church – should be confined to adults, rather than being administered to infants as in most Christian denominations. The word, originally used derisively by mainstream Christians, is derived from the Latin *anabaptismus* (second baptism), in turn from the Greek *ana*, meaning up or anew, and *baptismos* (baptism), and was first used in English in 1532. The second baptism would have been administered to adult converts who had already been baptised as infants. The Anabaptists were a radical wing of the 16th-century Reformation movement, seeking to model themselves on the earliest Christians. They rejected infant baptism on the grounds that infants had no knowledge of good and evil and could therefore not repent and accept baptism. They baptised converts for the first time in Zurich in 1525, in protest at the city council's decree that all unbaptised children be baptised. These particular Anabaptists, known as the Swiss Brethren, separated themselves from the control of the state church, thus becoming the first to practise the complete separation of church and state.

Anarchism A philosophy, literally meaning (from the Greek) "without rule", that holds that mankind can and should live in harmony without government – and that government is intrinsically harmful. The word was first used pejoratively in the 17th-century English civil war by opponents of the Levellers (a movement espousing popular sovereignty in opposition to the monarchy), but in 1793, while not using the word itself, a British journalist, William Godwin (1756–1836), elaborated on the virtues of anarchism and the natural goodness of human beings. The first to call himself an anarchist, in 1840, was the French philosopher Pierre-Joseph Proudhon (1809–65), famous for declaring that "property is theft". Anarchists are often linked with extreme left-wing movements and with Marxism, but – in contrast to anarchists – Marxists believe the state must first be taken over before it can wither away, hence a fundamental disagreement in the 19th century between Karl Marx (1818–83) and Mikhail Bakunin (1814–76), whose support for violent action inspired a string of political assassinations. Anarchism's high point was reached in the early decades of the 20th century in Europe, before it was crushed by the rise of fascism. It survives today only as a fringe movement, inspired by its opposition to globalisation (see globalism).

Anarcho-syndicalism A political and social movement, perhaps originating in the Spanish labour movement in the late 19th century but certainly common in France in the first decades of the 20th century, which sought to replace the state and establish in its place a society based on workers organised in units of production. The anarcho-syndicalists, who were influenced by Pierre-Joseph Proudhon (see anarchism), opposed the wage system as a form of exploitation by the capitalist class, reducing workers to the status of slaves. The derivation of the term is from the Greek *anarkhos*, meaning "without (*an*) a ruler (*arkhos*)", and the French *syndicalisme*, meaning trade unionism. The principles of anarcho-syndicalism were first spelled out at the "First

International" – the meetings of the International Workingmen's Association in the 1860s in London and Geneva – where participants were split into followers of Karl Marx and those, the anarchists, who preferred the views of his Russian rival Mikhail Bakunin. At the time, Marx favoured action through parliamentary democracy; Bakunin and his followers, in the words of another Russian revolutionary, Peter Kropotkin (1842–1921), advocated "direct economical struggle against capitalism, without interfering in the political parliamentary agitation". Though anarcho-syndicalism had widespread influence among workers in Europe (and, before the first world war, among America's workers, too), the movement faded after the first world war as trade unions and other workers' movements found the Soviet model of communism more convincing.

Aneurism An enlargement, also spelt as aneurysm, of a section of an artery caused by a weakening of the artery wall. The derivation is from the Greek *aneurusma*, meaning dilation or widening, and the wider the aneurism the greater the risk of rupture. If an aneurism of the aorta, the main artery from the heart, ruptures, there is a high risk of death.

Anglicanism A tradition of Christianity that has its roots in the Church of England (which rejected the authority of the Roman Catholic pope in 1534 in protest at the papal refusal to annul the marriage of Henry VIII). The word itself dates back only to the 19th century, adding a suffix to "Anglican", which dates back to the 13th century. By the Lambeth Conference of 1867 in London the sense of an "Anglican Communion" had emerged as a kind of middle way between **Roman Catholicism** and Reformed **Protestantism**. Anglicanism today has some 80m adherents and so is the largest Christian denomination after the Roman Catholic and Eastern Orthodox churches. Shared by all Anglicans, including America's Episcopalians, is the Book of Common Prayer. Anglican doctrine and practice are by no means strictly defined, with various strands coexisting in a "broad church". There is no single head of the Anglican Communion, but the Archbishop of Canterbury is considered "first among equals".

Animism   The belief (from the Latin *anima*, or "soul") that supernatural spirits, or souls, inhabit animals, plants or inanimate objects such as rocks. The British anthropologist Edward Burnett Tylor (1832–1917) first surveyed animistic beliefs in his 1871 book *Primitive Culture*, arguing that religion began with animism. The French sociologist Emile Durkheim (1858–1917) argued by contrast that religion began with **totemism**. While totemism and animism are similar, animism focuses on individual spirits that help sustain life, whereas totemism tends to emphasise ancestors, or the land itself, as the basis of life. Whatever the nuances, animism has been virtually universal in early cultures and remains widespread today. Japanese **Shintoism**, for example, is highly animistic, and animism is especially common in the developing world.

Antagonism A state of hostility or opposition, which may range from the petty to the serious and violent. In classical drama the antagonist is the adversary of the protagonist, or hero.

Anthropocentrism The theory that the world exists for the benefit of humans (*anthropos* being Greek for man), rather than animals. As such, the theory is generally reviled by environmentalists (see environmentalism), critical of the damage wrought by man's exploitation of the Earth.

Anthropomorphism The attribution of human characteristics or actions to a non-human object or being, especially to a god. The derivation is from the Greek *anthropos*, meaning man, and *morphe*, meaning form. The gods of ancient Greece were all to some extent anthropomorphised, but the most obvious modern examples are the depiction in Christian art of God as a bearded man and the attribution of human voices and personalities to Disney and other cartoon characters.

Anthroposophism (or anthroposophy) A philosophy that holds that the human intellect can contact the spiritual world. This idea (from the Greek *anthropos*, meaning man, and *sophia*, meaning wisdom) was developed by Rudolf Steiner (1861–1925), an Austrian philosopher and scientist, who proposed the existence of a spiritual world accessible to pure thought through an ability latent in all humans. Steiner said that man had participated in the spiritual processes of the world through a dreamlike consciousness – and could do so again by developing a faculty for thinking and perception separate from the senses. Steiner had originally been involved in the Theosophical Society but became disillusioned by the organisation's presentation of Jiddu Krishnamurti (1895–1986), an Indian religious philosopher, as the reincarnation of Christ. In 1912 Steiner founded the Anthroposophical Society, now based in Switzerland and with branches around the world.

Anti-Americanism A sentiment of hostility to the policies, culture or people of the United States. It is sometimes assumed that anti-Americanism began in the 20th century, as a reaction to the economic, technological and military supremacy of the United States and the parallel decline of European powers such as Britain and France. In fact, European anti-Americanism can be traced back at least to the 18th and 19th centuries, with the British writer Frances Trollope (1779–1863), for example, decrying America's "want of refinement". In the modern era, the Vietnam war and more recently the Iraq war have helped foment at times an almost universal opposition to American policy, with pollsters finding few positive views – despite America's continuing attraction as a destination for migrants and despite the global demand for American popular culture, from fashion to film. Degrees of anti-Americanism vary with place and time: French intellectuals have traditionally scorned America as crass; Muslims, regardless of country, criticise America's support for Israel and tend to regard its policy in the Middle East, Afghanistan and Pakistan as anti-Islamic.

Anti-capitalism A broad-brush term for opposition to the
economic system – capitalism – by which individuals
own the means of production and are free to maximise
their profits. Arguably, fascism is a form of anti-capitalism
since it welds corporatist interests with the state and so
reduces the freedom of the individual, but more obvious
opponents of capitalism are socialism and communism
(Marx predicted that capitalism would end because it
exploited the workers). There are, too, religious objections
to some aspects of capitalism: historically, the Roman
Catholic church forbade usury, and Islam similarly
forbids charging interest on loans. Though most
economists consider capitalism as the most effective
means of both increasing and distributing economic
growth, opponents frequently accuse it of harmful
excesses, be they lavish rewards for bankers and bosses
or damage to the environment in the quest for growth.

Anti-communism A 20th-century movement of opposition to
both the ideology of communism and, more particularly,
its practice by the Soviet Union and the People's Republic
of China. The Roman Catholic church was always
anti-communist. So too was the United States. But the
main opponents in the years in the first half of the
century were the fascist movements in Spain, Italy and
Germany. Germany's defeat in the second world war
ended the need for an American-Russian alliance and
marked the start of the "cold war" between the two
superpowers, each vying for ideological influence around
the world – hence war and conflict, directly or by proxy,
in Korea, South-East Asia, Africa, Afghanistan, the Middle

East and Latin America. Meanwhile, anti-communist
movements took root in European satellites of the Soviet
Union, from East Germany to Poland. With the collapse
of the Soviet Union in 1991 anti-communism lost much
of its reason for being – though not entirely: economic
hardship in central and eastern Europe in the 21st century
has led in some countries to a resurgence of communist
parties.

Antidisestablishmentarianism A 19th-century movement
seeking to preserve the Church of England's status as the
state church in England, Wales and Ireland (succeeding in
England, but failing in Wales and Ireland). The word now
survives in schoolroom lore as the (supposedly) longest
non-technical and non-scientific word in the English
language.

Anti-fascism A movement that opposed the rise of fascism in
western Europe in the 1920s and 1930s. One example was
the anti-Franco forces in the Spanish civil war of 1936–39;
another the French resistance to occupation by Nazi
Germany in the second world war. In Britain a notable
event was the "battle of Cable Street" in London's
working-class East End in 1936, when some 300,000
anti-fascist demonstrators clashed with some 10,000
police overseeing a march through the area by Oswald
Mosley's British Union of Fascists (Mosley was forced to
abandon the march). Before the collapse of the Soviet
Union, anti-fascism was often connected with
communism. Today it commands a wide spectrum of

political support, from anarchists (see anarchism) to liberal capitalists (see capitalism).

Anti-globalism Opposition to the process of globalisation (see globalism), and therefore opposition to the groups and institutions, from the International Monetary Fund to multinational corporations, that favour the process. The anti-globalism (or anti-globalisation) movement began in the late 20th century, at a time when America under Ronald Reagan (1911–2004) and Britain under Margaret Thatcher were advocating free markets and the dismantling of barriers to trade. The movement, intrinsically left-wing in its political stance, regularly holds mass demonstrations at international meetings – for example, at the Seattle meeting of the World Trade Organisation in 1999 and the G8 summit in Genoa in 2001. A bête noire of the movement is the annual World Economic Forum held in Davos, Switzerland. This has prompted the anti-globalism movement to hold a counter forum, the World Social Forum (its first meeting was in 2001 in Porto Alegre, Brazil).

Anti-imperialism As an opposition to the foreign conquests of great powers, anti-imperialism began in the late 19th century and grew in the 20th. The Anti-Imperialist League was formed in 1898 in Boston to oppose America's acquisition of the Philippines, and America's foreign reach in the 20th and 21st centuries has sustained an anti-American brand of anti-imperialism (see anti-Americanism). However, the greatest exponents of anti-imperialism were countries colonised by European powers such as Britain, France, Spain and Portugal. With the granting of independence to most of these colonies in the second half of the 20th century, anti-imperialism has waned. (See also **imperialism**.)

Antinomianism The doctrine that Christians are not obliged to obey moral or scriptural laws, especially those of the Old Testament (such as male circumcision), and that salvation is attained solely by faith and divine grace. This view allowed some heretical sects in early Christianity and in the Middle Ages to indulge in sexual licence, but antinomian views flourished during the Protestant Reformation in the 16th century and were held by strict and ascetic groups such as the Anabaptists (see **Anabaptism**) – though not by Martin Luther (1483–1546), who in 1539 wrote "Against the Antinomians" to refute the ideas of Johannes Agricola (1494–1566), the first in the Reformation era to hold that while non-Christians were subject to the laws of Moses, Christians were not, since they were answerable to the Gospel alone. Agricola, who subsequently recanted, argued that God treated the sinner with pity rather than wrath. Antinomianism remains a feature of several Protestant denominations, from the Mennonites and Anabaptists to the Quakers (for whom the "inner light" of God within each person takes precedence over the Scriptures – see **Quakerism**). The derivation of the term is from the Greek *anti*, meaning against, and *nomos*, meaning law.

Anti-Semitism Although Arabs, too, are Semitic, the term refers only to prejudice, hatred or persecution directed against Jews. As such it has a depressingly long history, from the Biblical tale of Exodus, through the medieval crusades and the various expulsions of Jews from Britain (in 1290), Spain (in 1492) and Portugal (in 1497) to the European pogroms of the 19th century and finally the Holocaust of the 20th century. Since the defeat of Hitler's Germany in 1945 anti-Semitism has receded but still commands some popular support, especially in Russia and former Soviet satellites. Explanations of anti-Semitism vary: some Christians blame Jews (the Old Testament-proclaimed "chosen people") for the death of Christ, and the ban on usury for Christians contributed to the oft-resented Jewish financial success. The Koran gives Jews a protected status, and historically Jews were much better treated in the Muslim world than in Europe. However, the creation of Israel in 1948 as a Jewish state has led to a widespread antagonism on the part of Muslims, with anti-Zionism (see Zionism) often turning into anti-Semitism.

Aphorism A succinct observation, or maxim, containing a supposed truth, such as "If it ain't broke, don't fix it" or Friedrich Nietzsche's "What does not destroy us makes us stronger". The term is from the Greek *aphorismos*, or definition, and was first applied to the collected sayings of the Greek physician Hippocrates (460–377BC), such as "Walking is man's best medicine" and "Life is short, art long, opportunity fleeting, experience misleading, judgment difficult".

Arianism A Christian heresy named after Arius (c250–336), a priest in Alexandria who claimed that Christ was not truly divine but was a supernatural being who was not quite human. Arius argued that God alone is self-existent and immutable; Christ the Son, created by God before all others, had a beginning and was finite – and so could not be immutable God. The Council of Nicaea in 325 condemned Arius as a heretic and proclaimed that the Son was "of one substance with the Father". Nevertheless, Arianism remained popular for the next half-century, especially during the reign, from 337 to 361, in the Roman empire of Constantius II, a convinced Arian. The collapse of Arianism came when the Christian emperors Gratian and Theodosius assumed power in the later part of the 4th century and when the First Council of Constantinople in 381 approved the Nicene creed and proscribed Arianism. The doctrine lived on in some Germanic tribes to the end of the 7th century, and is shared in large part today by Unitarians (see **Unitarianism**) and Jehovah's Witnesses.

Aristotelianism A school of philosophy based on the teachings of the classical Greek philosopher Aristotle (384–322BC). Aristotle studied with Plato, but whereas **Platonism** concentrates abstractly on idea as a precursor to matter, Aristotle emphasised empirical analysis and argued that all things have an inherent purpose. The idea, in Aristotelian teleology, that an explanation of something must consider its final cause or purpose, subsequently made Aristotelianism attractive to the Christian church, which could then identify purpose with

God's will and argue that since there is design in the world there must be a designer. Aristotelian ethics emphasise the intellect and the practice of virtue – which involves moderation. Aristotle's ideas, on subjects as varied as poetry and politics, have been influential through the ages, having been saved for the West by the translations into Arabic in the Middle Ages by Arab and Jewish scholars such as Al-Farabi and Maimonides.

Arminianism The theological doctrine of Jacobus Arminius (the Latinised name of Jakob Hermandszoon, 1560–1609), a Dutch Protestant, who contested some of the tenets of Calvinism. Whereas Calvin spoke of predestination and the total depravity of man and believed that salvation was entirely in God's gift, Arminius believed that man had free will and that faith was a man's contribution to his salvation. Similarly, whereas Calvin taught that it was God's choice of the sinner that led to salvation, Arminius taught that it was the sinner's choice of Christ. As such, Arminianism has been particularly influential in the growth of Methodism.

Asceticism A mode of living that limits or avoids earthly pleasures such as sex and alcohol. The notion, common to many religious traditions, is that such abstinence will help the attainment of spiritual goals (Buddhist ascetics, for example, seek nirvana – see Buddhism). Ironically, asceticism (from the Greek for "training") has a less elevated origin in the training regimes of athletes preparing for the Olympics in ancient Greece – and such disciplines remain fashionable in modern sport, making many an unspiritual boxer just as ascetic as a monk.

Atavism The reversion, as in "atavistic fears", to an earlier type, especially in the sense of ancestors or an earlier period of history. In biology, atavism (from the Latin *atavus*, or forefather) refers to the reappearance of the characteristics of a remote ancestor that have been absent in intervening generations. An atavism is thus an evolutionary throwback.

Atheism The belief that God or gods do not exist, in contrast to agnosticism, which leaves open the question. Atheism has been a common concept for centuries (Democritus and Epicurus were atheists in ancient Greece) and is explicit in Marxism (as Marx put it, "Religion is the opiate of the masses"). In the 19th century the German philosopher Friedrich Nietzsche (1844–1900) proclaimed "the death of God"; and in the 20th century the French philosopher Jean-Paul Sartre (1905–80) argued that human freedom and the existence of God were incompatible. Though atheism is usually described as unspiritual, some forms of Buddhism offer no gods and so their followers could technically be called atheists. The popularity of atheism is difficult to assess, but is certainly lower in America, where polls find that 75% of Americans believe in a supreme being, than in Europe (a 2006 poll reckoned 32% of the French were atheists).

Atomism The idea, developed by Leucippus and Democritus, Greek philosophers of the 5th century BC, that complex phenomena are collections of fixed units or atoms, and that changes come when the combinations of atoms change. In the early 20th century the British philosopher Bertrand Russell (1872–1970) and his Austrian pupil, Ludwig Wittgenstein (1889–1951), developed "logical atomism", a belief that the world consists ultimately of "facts", or atoms, that cannot be further broken down. Logical atomism attempts to identify the atoms of thought.

Authoritarianism A form of government that involves strong or even oppressive control of the people, but less so than the control exercised (often with force) by a totalitarian regime. The Roman Catholic church, for example, is authoritarian rather than totalitarian. Developing countries frequently have authoritarian governments, who argue that less control would mean lower economic growth.

Autism A lifelong development disorder characterised by difficulties in social interaction and communication and by obsessive and repetitive behaviour. The condition, usually apparent before a child is three years old, covers a broad spectrum of behaviour, and many sufferers – for example the so-called autistic savants – exhibit extraordinary talents in activities such as mathematics and music. A mild form of autism is Asperger syndrome. According to America's National Institutes of Health, three to six out of every thousand children are likely to be autistic, with boys four times more susceptible than girls.

b

Ba'athism The ideology of the Arab Socialist Ba'ath Party (*ba'ath* being the Arabic for renaissance). The Ba'ath Party was formed in the 1940s in Damascus by Michel Aflaq, a Syrian Christian, and Salah al-Din al-Bitar, a Muslim compatriot, and merged with the Syrian Socialist Party in 1953. Ba'athism espouses, at least in theory, non-alignment, pan-Arabism and anti-imperialism (in practice, Ba'athists aligned themselves with the Soviet Union during the cold war). Ba'athists have been in power in Syria since 1963, the same year in which they briefly took control in Iraq, regaining it there in 1968. Despite their shared and non-religious advocacy of Arab unity, the Syrian and Iraqi regimes never joined together. The Syrian branch of Ba'athism has survived under the authoritarian rule first of Hafez al-Assad and then of his son, Bashar. Ba'athism in Iraq ended in 2003 with the overthrow of Saddam Hussein (c1937–2006).

Babism A religion founded in Persia with a revelation experienced in 1844 by Mirza Ali Muhammad of Shiraz (1819–50), who announced himself as the Bab (Arabic for gate), meaning the gateway to the "hidden imam" of Shia Islam (in hiding since the 9th century) and so to the knowledge of God. In the same year Ali Muhammad gathered 18 disciples, who along with him added up to the sacred Babi number 19 (he also divided the year into 19 months of 19 days each). Ali Muhammad subsequently gave up the title of Bab and announced that he was in fact the 12th imam, and later he described himself as a manifestation of God. In 1848 the Babis declared a formal break with Islam, which served to worsen their conflicts with the established order and led to the arrest and execution in 1850 of Ali Muhammad. In 1867 the movement split, with one group – the Azalis – following the Bab's successor, Sobh-e Azal (1831–1912), and another Sobh-e Azal's half-brother, Baha'ullah, becoming known as Baha'is (the Bab remained for them a venerated figure).

Baha'ism A monotheistic religion founded in 19th-century Persia (now Iran) by Baha'ullah (1817–92) and continued by his eldest son, Abdu'l-Baha (1844–1921). Baha'ism (from the Arabic *baha'*, meaning splendour) has its roots in the teachings of Mirza Ali Muhammad, a preacher in Shiraz who was known as the Bab (Arabic for gate). The Bab, who was executed in Persia in 1850 and whose tomb in Haifa, Israel, is an important site for Baha'is, emphasised the notion of messianic messengers from God – of whom Baha'ullah claimed to be the latest example. Baha'ism stresses the oneness of mankind and of all religions, with God's truth progressively revealed by a succession of prophets, such as Abraham, Buddha, Jesus and Muhammad. One of the tenets of the faith is the equality

of men and women; another is the need to seek world
peace. There are perhaps 7m Baha'is around the world,
more than 2m of them in India. In Iran there remain
about 350,000 but they are the subject of persecution,
accused of being apostates from Islam.

Balkanism The process of dividing a region or country into
small and quarrelsome parts – or, by extension, a political
movement. The term comes from the troubled history of
Europe's Balkan peninsula, with wars in the late 19th
century and early 20th century as the Ottoman empire
disintegrated, and again in the late 20th century as
Yugoslavia disintegrated. These wars variously involved
Serbia, Greece, Albania, Macedonia, Montenegro, Bosnia,
Croatia, Kosovo, Turkey, Romania and Bulgaria.

Baptism The ritual, by sprinkling water onto a person's
forehead or immersing the person in water, that gives
admission to the Christian church. Almost invariably the
ceremony is accompanied by the Trinitarian invocation of
belief in the Father, the Son and the Holy Spirit. A form
of baptism exists in Judaism as the *mikvah*, a ritual
immersion to achieve purity (for example, by Orthodox
women after menstruation), and the New Testament
refers to John the Baptist – born a Jew – baptising Jesus.
Most early Christians were converts from Judaism or
paganism and so were baptised as adults, but the baptism
of infants was certainly common by the 2nd century and
is now the accepted custom of most Christian
denominations. Several Protestant churches, such as the
Baptists and Pentecostals, limit baptism to adults, on the

grounds that maturity is needed to make the profession of faith demanded by the ritual (for infant baptisms the profession of faith is normally made by the parents).

Behaviouralism The idea that political science – as with the natural sciences – should restrict itself to independently observable and quantifiable behaviour, for example through the study of society and culture and through opinion polls.

Behaviourism A theory of learning that emphasises only objectively observable behaviour and so discounts the hypothesis of the mind. Learning, therefore, is simply the acquisition of new behaviour. The Russian psychologist Ivan Pavlov (1849–1936), with his ideas of conditioning, can be considered a behaviourist, as was B.F. Skinner (1904–90), an American psychologist.

Bicameralism The more usual meaning is a system of government involving the coexistence (harmonious or otherwise) of two legislative bodies, such as the Senate and the House of Representatives in America or the House of Lords and the House of Commons in Britain. A second meaning is a theory proposed in 1976 by Julian Jaynes (1920–97), an American psychologist, that at one point in human development one part of the brain "spoke" to another, which in turn listened and obeyed. Ancient man would therefore experience his environment rather as a schizophrenic might today.

Bilateralism A process, particularly in international relations, involving two sides – usually countries. Bilateralism is the narrowest form of collaboration on a spectrum that would go as wide as multilateralism (the spectrum would begin with unilateralism, where there is obviously no collaboration). Economists dislike bilateralism in trade agreements on the grounds that it leads to a plethora of accords that may conflict with each other.

Bimetallism A monetary system based on the circulation of currencies in two metals, traditionally gold and silver, at a fixed ratio (and so rate of exchange) to each other. Bimetallic systems were common to most countries by the end of the 18th century (American coinage, for example, had the gold eagle and the silver dollar). In 1865 France, Belgium, Italy and Switzerland formed the Latin Monetary Union, establishing bimetallism on an international scale, but the system was undermined by the monetary manipulations of Italy and Greece (a later member of the union) and collapsed during the Franco-German war of 1870–71). One advantage of bimetallism is that it provides a bigger monetary base than would be the case with just one metal. Problems occur, however, when the ratio in the official prices of gold and silver differs from the ratio available in the open market – leading to an instance of "Gresham's Law". This is a phenomenon coined by Henry Dunning Macleod (1821–1902), a Scottish economist, in 1858 in homage to Sir Thomas Gresham (1519–79), a financial adviser to Queen Elizabeth I. Gresham noted that "good and bad coin cannot circulate together" (in other words, the money with a higher intrinsic value – such as gold coin – will be hoarded and eventually driven out of circulation by the money with lesser intrinsic value).

Black nationalism A movement among black Americans in the 1960s and 1970s, derived from Marcus Garvey's Universal Negro Improvement Association of the early 20th century, that sought to engender communal pride and gain political and economic power. Using slogans such as "black power" and "black is beautiful", black nationalists emphasised an identity separate from that of overwhelmingly white America; some, indeed, looked forward to a separate African-American nation. One prominent black nationalist was Malcolm X (1925–65) of the "Nation of Islam", who called for a "black revolution" and derided the efforts of civil rights' leaders such as Martin Luther King (1929–68) to integrate blacks into the American mainstream. After a pilgrimage to Mecca in 1964, Malcolm X abandoned the idea of racial separation but still advocated black self-reliance.

Blairism The political ideology of Tony Blair, leader of Britain's Labour Party (1994–2007) and Britain's prime minister from 1997 to 2007. Blair, who helped renovate the Labour Party to become what he and his allies called "New Labour", espoused the so-called "Third Way", promoted by thinkers such as Anthony Giddens, to transcend the division between left-wing socialism and right-wing capitalism. In practice, this meant combining elements of left and right economic policies, for example pouring money into the public health sector and education while simultaneously introducing into them the pressures of the market. In foreign policy, Blairism meant initially a favourable attitude towards the European Union and, consistently, an Atlanticist policy of supporting America, be it under the Democratic administration of Bill Clinton or the Republican administration of his successor, George W. Bush. The Blairite alliance with America led to Britain's involvement in the Iraq invasion of 2003 and the toppling of Saddam Hussein (c1937–2006), the aftermath of which has encouraged many, on both left and right, to scorn Blairism.

Bogomilism The doctrine of a dualist religious sect that flourished in the Balkans from the 10th to 15th centuries. The movement began in Bulgaria in the mid-10th century and was named after its founder, a priest named Bogomil ("dear to God" in Bulgarian). The Bogomils had a Manichaean view of the world, believing that the material world was the creation of the devil (see Manichaeism). They therefore denied the Christian doctrine of incarnation and all the rites of the prevailing Orthodox church. Bogomilism, characterised by extreme austerity, condemned contact with worldly matters, especially marriage, the eating of meat and the drinking of wine. It spread through much of the Byzantine empire during the 11th and 12th centuries, fed by a nationalist Slavic opposition to oppression by the Orthodox church and by memories of the forced Christian conversion of the Slavs by Tsar Boris I of Bulgaria after 863. Indeed, in Bosnia Bogomilism was embraced by the rulers.

Elsewhere, persecution grew and though the Bogomils remained powerful in Bulgaria until the late 14th century, they faded into insignificance with the Ottomans' 14th-century defeat of the Byzantine empire and their conquest of south-eastern Europe.

Bohemianism A term used to describe a casual, unconventional lifestyle, free from the fetters of mainstream society. The word was first used in connection with artists and writers in 19th-century France. The allusion was to roving gypsies, who were supposed to have arrived from the central European region of Bohemia. More modern bohemianism can be seen in the western world's hippies and "beat generation" of the 1960s. A more recent phenomenon in France is the appearance of the *bobo* – an abbreviation of *bourgeois bohème* that signified an affectation by the affluent of bohemianism in manners and dress.

Bolshevism The doctrine and strategy of the followers of Vladimir Ilych Lenin (1870–1924) – the Bolsheviks – in seizing power and establishing a "dictatorship of the proletariat". The Bolshevik Party, from the Russian word for majority, in contrast to the Mensheviks (the minority) in the competing strains of **communism**, was established in 1912 when the Bolshevik and Menshevik factions of the Russian Social-Democratic Workers' Party (RSDWP) formally split into separate parties. The Bolsheviks had gained their name from the second congress of the RSDWP in 1903, at which they argued that party membership be restricted to professional revolutionaries,

winning for themselves a temporary majority on the
party's central committee and on the editorial board of its
newspaper. Whereas the Mensheviks were open to
alliances with liberal Russians and a gradual path to
socialism, the characteristics of Bolshevism were a
commitment to world revolution and a belief in
"democratic centralism". In Lenin's words, this meant
"freedom of discussion, unity of action" – in reality a
recipe for the dictatorship of Joseph Stalin that followed
the Russian revolution of October 1917 (see Stalinism).
During the first world war the Bolsheviks hoped for the
defeat of tsarist Russia and the development of an
international civil war (the Mensheviks were divided
between a right wing that supported Russia's war effort
and a left that argued for pacifism). In the aftermath of
the 1917 revolution the Bolsheviks became increasingly
powerful, and in 1918 changed their name to the Russian
Communist Party. In 1925 this became the All-Union
Communist Party – which in 1952 became the
Communist Party of the Soviet Union. (For their part, the
Mensheviks were finally suppressed in 1921.)

Bonapartism In terms of history, the political movement to
restore 19th-century France and its empire to the family of
Napoleon Bonaparte (Napoleon I) and his nephew
Louis-Napoleon (Napoleon III), with Napoleon viewed
not just as a political and military genius but as the
defender of the common man. In modern terms, the
word refers to the preference for a strong, centralised state
based on popular support. Marx saw Bonapartism as a
way in which a narrow ruling class could co-opt a

revolution, with both Napoleon I and Napoleon III
having corrupted French revolutions: "History repeats
itself, first as tragedy, then as farce."

Botulism A rare, paralysing disease of the nervous system
caused by consuming canned meats and other preserved
foods poisoned by the *Clostridium botulinum* bacterium.
The word, originating in the late 19th century, comes from
the German *Botulismus* (meaning sausage poisoning), first
identified in 1897 by Emile van Ermengem (1851–1932), a
Belgian bacteriologist. The German word in turn comes
from the Latin *botulus*, or sausage. Ironically, the
botulinum toxin, known by the trade name Botox, is now
used as a cosmetic alternative to surgery in removing
wrinkles.

Bruxism The involuntary habit of grinding the teeth,
normally during sleep. Bruxism, derived from the Greek
brukhein, or "gnash the teeth", and first used in the 1930s,
is often associated with stress.

Buddhism A philosophy and, for many, a religion founded by
Siddhartha Gautama (the Buddha, or "enlightened one")
in north-east India in the 6th century BC. Buddhists, who
number nearly 380m around the world, do not believe in
any god but in the "four noble truths": life is suffering;
suffering is a result of one's desires; to stop suffering one
must stop desiring; and the way to stop desiring is the
"noble eightfold path" – correct views, intention, speech,
conduct, livelihood, effort, mindfulness and
concentration. In other words, through ethical conduct

and discipline (often involving meditation) a Buddhist can eventually reach the perfect peace of nirvana, or "blowing out" – the state of being freed from suffering and the cycle of rebirth. There are several Buddhist traditions, the main ones being the Theravada, popular in south-east Asia and emphasising meditation and self-liberation through one's own efforts, and Mahayana, a collection of schools such as Zen (which strives to understand the meaning of life without the intervention of logic and language) and Pure Land (which emphasises chanting). The Mahayana schools are dominant in Tibet, China, Mongolia, Korea and Japan.

Bushism Any of many unintentionally funny remarks by George W. Bush as America's 43rd president – for example, "Families is where our nation finds hope, where wings take dream"; "I know the human being and fish can coexist peacefully"; and "Our enemies are innovative and resourceful, and so are we. They never stop thinking about new ways to harm our country and our people, and neither do we."

Butskellism A term coined by *The Economist* in 1954 to describe the common approach to economic and social policy of two successive British chancellors of the exchequer (chief finance ministers), Hugh Gaitskell (Labour, 1950–51) and R.A. ("Rab") Butler (Conservative, 1951–55). Both men favoured a Keynesian "mixed economy", with a strong welfare state and moderate state intervention designed to increase employment and improve education and health care (see **Keynesianism**).

C

Calvinism A set of beliefs in Protestant Christianity, originating in the doctrines of a 16th-century French theologian and pastor, John Calvin (born Jean Cauvin, 1509–64). Calvinism has five essential points: "total depravity", meaning that everyone is born sinful; predestination for those – "the elect" – chosen by God; atonement for those sinners who are to be saved (Christ, according to Calvinism, did not die to save all sinners); "irresistible grace", meaning that the elect cannot resist God's call; and the perseverance of the saints, meaning that those chosen for salvation will reach heaven. As Calvin gloomily put it, God preordained "a part of the human race, without any merit of their own, to eternal salvation, and another part, in just punishment of their sin, to eternal damnation."

Cannibalism In zoological terms, the eating of one member of a species by another; and in common parlance, the practice of humans eating other humans (also known as anthropophagy). Tales of cannibalism can be found throughout history, even back to ancient Egypt (the god

Osiris apparently gave the Kemites crops to prevent cannibalism). Today such tales tend to involve tribes in Papua New Guinea, and there are stories of soldiers in African conflicts eating their enemies' organs. How reliable such accounts are is a matter of debate, given both the prejudices of colonialism and the stigma of cannibalism. What is clear is that cannibalism has frequently been the salvation of starving and desperate humans – not least for the surviving passengers of an aircraft crash in the Andes in 1972. One 19th-century case of cannibalism, when three shipwrecked sailors killed and ate an ailing fourth in order to survive their journey in a lifeboat, resulted in the conviction for murder of Tom Dudley and Edwin Stephens in 1884 and set a precedent in British common law that necessity is no defence against a charge of murder (the eventual punishment of Dudley and Stephens was six months' imprisonment).

Capitalism An economic system in which the means of production are privately owned and production is guided and profits are distributed through free markets operating according to the price signals set by demand and supply. Karl Marx argued that capitalism exploited labour and so would eventually and inevitably be overthrown (see Marxism). So far he has been wrong, despite periodic faults, from high unemployment and yawning income disparities to environmental degradation, attributed to capitalism by its critics. Defenders of capitalism argue that it is the most efficient creator of wealth for all that the world has ever seen, and point out that in modern capitalism each worker owns – and so can sell – his own labour. Capitalism grew from the 16th century onwards in Europe as a successor to feudalism, but the best advocate of modern capitalism has undoubtedly been Adam Smith (1723–90) with his 1776 book *An Inquiry into the Nature and Causes of the Wealth of Nations*, which said economic decisions were best set by self-regulating market forces. Also crucial to the theory of capitalism was the British economist David Ricardo (1772–1823), who in the 19th century promulgated the "law of comparative advantage", explaining why it is profitable for two parties to trade with each other even if one of them is superior in all forms of production. For all the strengths of capitalism, it proved unable to forestall the Wall Street crash of 1929 and the subsequent Great Depression of the 1930s. One consequence was the theory of Keynesianism, emphasising the need for government spending when private investment falls short. In the 1970s and 1980s Keynesianism fell out of favour, supplanted by monetarism – though this change of fortune proved temporary, as Keynes's ideas once again seemed relevant as a remedy for the credit crunch of 2009.

Careerism The desire to advance one's career, even to the detriment of other interests and other people.

Catastrophism The theory that changes in the Earth's crust and the differences in fossil forms in successive geological strata are the result of cataclysmic events, rather than a gradual process of incremental change (as in uniformitarianism and gradualism). The leading proponent of catastrophism was the French naturalist and

paleontologist Georges Cuvier (1769–1832), whose ideas
were then linked by British geologists of the time to the
Biblical account of Noah's Ark and the flood – though
Cuvier himself, as a man of the Enlightenment, never
made such creationist claims (see creationism). A
20th-century refinement of Cuvier's views, known as
neocatastrophism, explains geological history as a slow
sequence of rhythms leading to abrupt change, including
the extinction of some organisms.

Catechism A written manual of religious information, often
in the form of questions and answers, to instruct
believers, especially the young, in their faith (almost
invariably Christian). Catechisms have existed since
medieval times and became popular after the invention
of printing in the 15th century.

Catharism The doctrine of the Cathars, a heretical Christian
sect in western Europe (especially the Languedoc region
of France) that flourished in the 12th and 13th centuries
and professed a form of Manichean dualism – the
presence of good and evil, with man an alien being in a
material world that was evil. The Cathars (from the Greek
katharoi, meaning pure) shared this view with other
medieval sects, such as the Paulicians in Armenia and the
Bogomils in Bulgaria (see Bogomilism). By the middle of
the 12th century the Cathar church was well established
in France, including at Albi – hence the common
description of southern French Cathars as Albigensians
(see Albigensianism). In theory, the doctrine was
extremely ascetic, with sexual intercourse forbidden

– and yet it became popular by dint of dividing its followers between the "perfect", who abided by the strict moral standard, and the "believers", who were not expected to attain the same standard. A conflict with the Roman Catholic church, however, became inevitable, since the Cathars considered Jesus to be not God incarnate but merely an angel, whose human sufferings and death were an illusion. The result was a series of papal wars – such as the Albigensian crusade – against the Cathars in southern France, breaking their power by the mid-13th century. The Cathars went underground; their hierarchy collapsed during the 1270s; and their doctrine finally disappeared early in the 15th century.

Catholicism From the Greek word for "universal", the belief and practices of the Christian church based on the "apostolic succession", or a lineage that goes back to the 12 apostles of Christ. The word may refer either to the Roman Catholic church, led by the Pope in Rome (**Roman Catholicism**), or, less usually, to those denominations that consider themselves part of the Catholic church before its split into the Latin (western) and Greek (eastern) traditions. Anglicans consider their church to be Catholic despite their refusal to acknowledge papal supremacy.

Centralism The policy of putting a state or organisation under central control. "Democratic centralism" was the policy in communist countries by which local bodies elected representatives to a higher body whose decisions were then to be respected by the local bodies. The theory was that this allowed for democratic input ("freedom of discussion, unity of action", in Lenin's words). In practice, such input was rare, with local organisations almost invariably following dictates from above.

Charlatanism The state of being a fraudster. Charlatans have existed throughout history, spawning many descriptive nouns, from conmen in finance to quacks in medicine.

Chartism A working-class campaign for parliamentary reform in Britain, named after "The People's Charter". This was a manifesto drawn up in 1838, a time of economic depression, by William Lovett (1800–77), a London radical who had founded the London Working Men's Association two years earlier. The charter contained six demands: universal male suffrage; equal electoral districts; voting by ballot; an annually elected Parliament; payment of Parliament's members; and the abolition of the property qualification for membership of Parliament. As the movement took on a national scale, largely thanks to the rhetoric and leadership of an Irishman, Feargus O'Connor (c1796–1855), the Chartists held a "People's Parliament" in London in 1839. But their petition was rejected by the real Parliament (as was another in 1842), and violence between the Chartists in Wales and the army led to the arrest of most Chartist leaders, and the deportation of some. The final petition by the Chartists was in 1848 – a year of bad harvests in Britain and revolution in Europe – and was again rejected. As Victorian Britain began to prosper, Chartism faded – though, of course, all its goals were subsequently achieved.

Chauvinism Unreasoning and extreme patriotism, equivalent to jingoism and derived from the name of Nicolas Chauvin, a retired (and possibly mythical) French soldier who, despite poverty and disability, remained fanatically devoted in the early 19th century to the deposed Emperor Napoleon. The word has enjoyed a revival in recent years thanks to the coining of the phrase "male chauvinism" by feminists (see feminism) in the 1960s to describe the tendency of men to consider themselves the superior sex.

Christianism A belief not just in the tenets of Christianity but in its superiority. The word is of recent vintage and, as with Islamism when describing Islam, suggests fundamentalism and extremism.

Chromaticism The use of notes alien to the diatonic scale of a musical composition to add colour to the melody.

Chromatism The state of being coloured. In medicine, chromatism (from the Greek *khroma*, meaning colour) refers to an abnormal pigmentation.

Classicism An artistic and cultural tradition, first flourishing with the Italian Renaissance of the 14th–16th centuries, of admiration for ancient, or classical, Greece and Rome. Classicism, which emphasises the characteristics of harmony and restraint, is often used interchangeably with neoclassicism, the intentional imitation from the 18th century onwards of the classical period.

Cognitivism A theory of psychology that compares the mind to a "black box" or computer, with the learner receiving and processing information. Whereas behaviourism holds that actions are the result of external stimuli, cognitivism regards actions as the consequence of thinking. In the field of ethics, cognitivism is a theory that holds that sentences are propositions and so can be either true or false.

Collectivism The opposite of individualism. The concept, namely that the collective (normally the state) should take precedence over the individual, was explored by Jean-Jacques Rousseau (1712–78), Georg Hegel (1770–1831) and Karl Marx and is intrinsic not just to socialism and communism but also to fascism. Examples of collectivism in practice include collective farms, social housing and Israeli kibbutzim. Collectivism has frequently disappointed its advocates, with collective farming proving disastrously inefficient in communist China and with social housing in developed countries often blighted by high crime rates.

Colonialism The practice of establishing colonies in a foreign territory, thereby involving the subjugation of the native people by the colonisers. Colonialism is doubtless a phenomenon almost as old as history, but it is normally associated with the imperial expansion into Africa, Asia and the Americas from the 15th century onwards of European powers such as Portugal, Britain, Spain, France, Belgium, Holland, Germany and Italy. Apologists for colonialism cite the benefits often provided (for example, by the British in India) of law and order; critics decry the economic exploitation and cruelty often connected with colonisation (witness the Belgian Congo). Colonialism virtually disappeared with the wave of decolonisation in the 20th century, only to be replaced, say some, by neocolonialism, with the strong exercising their power by economic rather than military means.

Commercialism The spirit of commerce, normally in a derogatory sense, as in "commercialism has destroyed the meaning of Christmas".

Communalism A form of political and social organisation based on the commune, or self-contained community of people living together, with the state then becoming a confederation of communes. An implication of communalism is the sharing of property and responsibilities, and the association is often made with socialism and communism (and, indeed, anarchism). A rather different meaning for communalism is allegiance to the interests of a particular ethnic or religious group rather than to those of society as a whole.

Communism A political and social system envisaging a classless society in which property and the means of production are owned by the community rather than, as in capitalism, by individuals. Such ideas have been traced back two millennia to Christ's "Sermon on the Mount" and to Thomas More's 16th-century book *Utopia*, but as a political ideology – frequently interchangeable at the time with socialism – communism came of age in 19th-century

Europe, heir to the French Revolution of 1789 and a reaction to industrialisation, which was creating a new and poor urban working class. In 1848 Karl Marx (1818–83) and Friedrich Engels (1820–95) published *The Communist Manifesto*: communism would be the final stage of a process in which class differences would be eliminated; socialism, in which some class differences remained, was an intermediate stage in the process and to reach communism there would first have to be a revolutionary "dictatorship of the proletariat".

Communism achieved political power with the victory of Vladimir Lenin and his Bolsheviks in the Russian revolution of 1917 (see **Bolshevism**). Marx and Engels, declaring that "the working class has no country", had urged "Proletarians of all countries, unite". Between the first and second world wars much of Europe was riven by the competing ideologies of **fascism** and communism, with Russia, for example, providing moral and financial support for the anti-Franco Republicans in the Spanish civil war of the 1930s. But the communists' real success came in the aftermath of the second world war, when most of central and eastern Europe became satellite states of Joseph Stalin's Union of Soviet Socialist Republics. Similar triumphs came in Asia, with the 1949 revolutionary victory in China of the Chinese Communist Party under Mao Zedong (1893–1976) and the subsequent spread of communist rule to North Korea, Vietnam, Laos and Cambodia. Elsewhere in the so-called cold war, Fidel Castro in 1959 led a successful communist coup in Cuba.

Despite the high ideals of communism, in practice it has invariably meant authoritarian or repressive rule by the state and economic incompetence – hence the eventual collapse of communism in Europe in 1989 and the collapse two years later of the Soviet Union. By the start of the 21st century only China, North Korea, Vietnam, Laos and Cuba boasted communist regimes, but China and Vietnam in particular have introduced capitalist reforms to their economies.

Communitarianism A political and social movement that emerged in the late 20th century to argue that an individual's rights must be balanced by that same individual's responsibilities to society (or the community). The movement, espoused by sociologists such as the Israeli-American Amitai Etzioni, criticised an excess of individualism in liberal democracies and had a passing influence in the 1990s on the governments of Bill Clinton in America and Tony Blair in Britain.

Conformism The habit of being conventional in behaviour or thought, often implying a lack of individual initiative. Nonconformism usually refers to Protestants in England and Wales who refuse to conform to the authority and customs of the Church of England (such Protestants include Presbyterians, Quakers, Baptists, Congregationalists and Methodists).

Confucianism An ethical system derived from the teachings of Confucius, or Kung Fu Tzu (551–479BC), which emphasise the virtues of love within the family (duties within the family extend to the veneration of ancestors), honesty, righteousness and loyalty to the state. Crucial to Confucianism, which underlies the major cultures of East Asia, is the concept of the "noble man", embodying "the qualities of saint, scholar and gentleman" and acting as a moral guide. One feat attributed to Confucianism was the creation in China two millennia ago of a civil service chosen on merit. In recent times Singapore's leaders have praised Confucianism as the foundation of the "Asian values" that they see as fundamental to economic development and social stability in East Asia. Western critics connect Confucianism with the acceptance of paternalistic and authoritarian government.

Congregationalism A strand of Protestant Christianity, beginning in the late 16th century in Britain and then spreading to America, in which each congregation organises and governs its own affairs. The result is that there are no bishops, as in the Church of England, or elders as in the Presbyterian church, each individual church being independent and autonomous. The Congregationalist system of governance is also common in Muslim mosques and Jewish synagogues.

Consequentialism The doctrine in ethics and philosophy that actions should be judged on the basis of their consequences rather than their conformity to rules or obligations. The doctrine is closely linked to classical utilitarianism, which argues that an action is good or bad depending on the net balance it gives in the universe of pleasure over pain. The consequentialism of the British philosopher George Edward Moore (1873–1958) was "ideal utilitarianism", recognising that beauty and friendship are goods that actions should aim to maximise. The consequentialism of Richard Mervyn Hare (1919–2002), another British philosopher, was "preferential utilitarianism", arguing that an action is right if it maximises the satisfaction of a desire, no matter what the desire is. Consequentialism stands in contrast to deontology (see **deontologism**), in which the rightness or otherwise of an action stems from the nature of the action itself. The term "consequentialism" was coined by yet another British philosopher, Elizabeth Anscombe (1919–2001), in her 1958 essay *Modern Moral Philosophy*.

Conservatism The political ideology of those who value conserving the present order, with a belief in traditions and institutions that have stood the test of time. Change, therefore, should be gradual and infrequent. In practice, conservatives position themselves on the centre-right of the political spectrum, opposed to the left-wing's desire for social change and emphasising private property and institutions such as the church and the family. The birthplace of modern conservatism was Britain, and its father was the parliamentarian Edmund Burke (1729–97). Burke developed his ideas in reaction to what he saw as the folly of the French Revolution. He did not disagree with the "rights" proclaimed by the revolutionaries – "They are metaphysically true," he said – but thought they were too abstract to be used as the structure of governance. The duty of a government, in Burke's view, was to act out of practical – not idealistic – considerations.

This view underlay the rise, from the 1830s, of the Conservative Party in Britain and of similar parties elsewhere in Europe and in America (where the Republicans are the equivalent of the British Conservatives). Ironically, in the late 20th century Britain under Margaret Thatcher's leadership and America under Ronald Reagan (1911–2004) both experienced what has been called "radical conservatism", with their societies undergoing dramatic change.

Constructivism A theory of learning, based on the work of the 20th-century Swiss philosopher Jean Piaget (1896–1980), that holds that we construct our understanding of the world by reflecting on our experiences. Learning is the process of adjusting our mental picture of the world to make sense of our experiences. In the world of art, constructivism was a style that began in Russia in 1914 with the geometric constructions of Vladimir Tatlin (1885–1953). In 1920 Tatlin, joined by Antoine Pevsner (1886–1962) and Pevsner's brother, Naum Gabo (1890–1977), published the *Realist Manifesto*, urging artists to "construct" their work, using machinery and industrial materials. In mathematics, constructivism is a theory that treats a mathematical statement as true only if there is a proof of it, the idea being that it is necessary to "construct" a mathematical object to prove its existence. The term "constructivism" can be used in a variety of contexts: for example, social constructivism refers to how human interactions result in social phenomena; similarly constructivism in international relations refers to the political consequences of social interactions (arguing, for example, that power politics is not ordained by nature but is constructed by societies).

Consumerism The practice of emphasising consumption as an economic virtue – which is why critics, especially of globalisation, link consumerism to excessive and "conspicuous" consumption. Consumerism is doubtless ages old, but in popular usage, beginning in the 1960s, refers to western capitalism.

Corporatism A political doctrine, originating in the 19th century, in which various interest groups, such as business or farming or labour, are represented in a state's governing or legislative structure. This "functional representation" arose as a counter to the trend in the western world to either universal suffrage or independent trade unionism. After the first world war the fascist regimes of Italy, Spain, Germany and Portugal, as well as Vichy France, endorsed corporative forms of representation (see fascism), but the reality was authoritarian or dictatorial government. A more benign form of corporatism was the functional constituencies in the Hong Kong legislature under British rule. In popular usage corporatism is generally derided as political lobbying by big business.

Cosmopolitanism The view that all people in the world are members of a single community (and should not therefore be limited by the parochial notions of patriotism and nationalism). The idea of cosmopolitanism (*kosmos* is the Greek for world and *polis* for city) goes

back to classical Greece in the 4th century BC, when
Diogenes, rather than expressing any special link to his
city of Sinope, declared: "I am a citizen of the world
(*kosmopolites*)."

Creationism The belief, notably by fundamentalist Christians
(but also by some Jews and Muslims from their reading
of the Torah and the Koran), that the world was created
by God and literally as described in the Book of Genesis
– that is, in a period of six days. "Young Earth"
creationists hold that the world was created just 6,000
years ago; "Old Earth" creationists put the date some
billions of years ago. Creationism is as old as all the
Abrahamic religions, but became a matter of political
sensitivity in the 20th century when virtually all
scientists embraced Charles Darwin's theory of
evolution. Creationism has remained stubbornly popular
in many southern states of America (indeed, in 1925 in
Tennessee a biology teacher, John Thomas Scopes, was
found guilty by a court of the crime of teaching
evolution), but in 1987 the Supreme Court ruled that
teaching creationism in schools violated the constitution's
separation of church and state. Nonetheless, opinion
polls consistently attribute a belief in creationism to more
than two-fifths of Americans. (See also **fundamentalism**.)

Cubism A style of art originating in Europe in the early 20th
century in works by Pablo Picasso (1881–1973) and
Georges Braque (1882–1963). The term was first used in
1908 by a French art critic, Louis Vauxcelles (1870–1945).
Cubist paintings eschew the traditional use of perspective

in favour of flat, two-dimensional images, in which the subject is seen simultaneously from many different angles.

Cynicism Originally, the doctrine of the Cynics, philosophers in 5th-century BC Greece who followed Antisthenes and believed the purpose of life was to follow the path of virtue in harmony with nature. In practice, this meant living a life free from the constraints of convention (Diogenes, for example, lived in a barrel). The modern definition of cynicism, found in the 18th-century writings of satirists such as Jonathan Swift (1667–1745), is one of scepticism concerning the motives of others. In the words of Oscar Wilde (1854–1900), a cynic is "a man who knows the price of everything and the value of nothing".

d

Dadaism A cultural movement, originating in 1916 in Zurich, that reacted against the barbarism of the first world war, viewing traditional "bourgeois" art as being complicit in that war. Dadaism, described by its followers as "anti-art", attracted artists such as the French Marcel Duchamp (1887–1968) and the German Max Ernst (1891–1976). Its influence spread also to literature, with the German Kurt Schwitters (1887–1948), for example, composing "sound poems" and several composers writing "Dada" music. Dadaism was in many ways a forerunner of surrealism – and also of punk.

Darbyism The doctrines of John Nelson Darby (1800–82), an Anglo-Irish evangelist whose teachings were adopted by the Plymouth Brethren, a strict sect of Protestant Christianity that has no clergy or hierarchy and believes the Anglican church has strayed from the original traditions of Christianity. Darby preached the notion of dispensationalism, an interpretation of the Bible involving a historical progression of God's revelations and plan for salvation, a millenarian prediction of the imminent second coming of Christ and the certainty of the "rapture", when those who are saved will be transported to heaven.

Darwinism The theory of natural selection and evolution developed by the 19th-century British scientist Charles Darwin (1809–82). The term was coined by Thomas Huxley in his 1860 review of Darwin's *On the Origin of Species*. Darwin argued that evolution involves the interaction of variation (present in all forms of life), heredity and the struggle for existence. This struggle for existence decides which variations will be advantageous in a given environment, so altering the species through selective reproduction. The term "Darwinism" subsequently embraced evolutionary theory beyond Darwin himself in both biology and society. "Social Darwinism", for example, was developed by a British philosopher, Herbert Spencer (1820–1903), in the Victorian era to argue for the survival of the fittest, the implication being that the poor and weak did not deserve help. Whereas Darwinism did not distinguish between acquired characteristics (which cannot be inherited) and genetic variations (which can be passed from one generation to the next), modern knowledge of genetics, especially of gene mutation, which can explain how variations arise, has supplemented Darwinism in a theory known as neo-Darwinism.

Decentralism The idea, as in decentralisation, of dispersing power from the centre to local communities. One alleged benefit is to create a human scale, in contrast to the giant scale of much of modern life. As the German economist E.F. Schumacher (1911–77) put it: "Small is beautiful."

Deconstructionism An approach to linguistic analysis, originating in the work of the French philosopher Jacques Derrida (1930–2004), that "deconstructs" the ideological and other assumptions inherent in a text. Intrinsic to this concept – baffling to many – is the notion that individual experiences will challenge commonly accepted "ultimate truths". Derrida rejected the idea that understanding something requires an acquaintance with its meaning, directly present in our consciousness. This notion, he argued, involved "the myth of presence", whereas understanding something requires an idea of the ways in which it relates to other things, and the ability to recognise it in different contexts. Derrida coined the word *différance* in French, to combine "difference" and "deferral" and show that language is an infinite "play of *différance*", infinitely unstable.

Defeatism The attitude of accepting, or being resigned to, defeat. Lenin coined the concept of "revolutionary defeatism", arguing that the ruling classes sent the lower classes to fight for them in a capitalist war – but that the workers would actually be better off if their nations were defeated, thus preparing the way for international revolution.

Deism A belief in God (the Latin *deus*) based on reason and observation rather than on any divine revelation. As such, deism is fundamentally different from **Judaism**,

Christianity and Islam, all of which rely on revelations transmitted through prophets. Deists argue that God created the universe but then left it to operate under the laws of nature that he had devised. Deism appealed to many European and American thinkers during the 18th century "Enlightenment". However, deism – by denying God's intervention in the world – offends today's fundamentalist Christians (see **fundamentalism**).

Deontologism The theory, based on the work of the German philosopher Immanuel Kant (1724–1804), that only acts carried out from a sense of duty have moral value, "duty for duty's sake" being the moral imperative. An act must be judged by its intrinsic moral value rather than by its consequences.

Despotism The exercise of absolute authority by a single ruler or governing group. In other words, tyranny.

Determinism A philosophical theory, much debated by 19th-century thinkers such as the British philosopher John Stuart Mill (1806–73), that holds that man's wishes and even actions are determined by pre-existing circumstances and the laws of nature. Free will, therefore, is not as free as we like to imagine.

Dialectical materialism The Marxist theory that historical events are the consequence of the conflict of opposites, so, philosophically, a thesis and an antithesis result in a synthesis. The theory, which was adopted as the official philosophy of the Soviet Union, comes from the view of

Karl Marx and Friedrich Engels – itself derived from the philosophy of the German Georg Hegel (1770–1831) – that the material world has an objective reality independent of the mind. In this view, materialism is the opposite of idealism, which Marx and Engels saw as a theory in which matter was dependent on the mind or spirit. Derived from the notion of dialectical materialism is the theory of historical materialism, arguing that history should be interpreted in terms of a class struggle, pitting capitalists (see capitalism) and landowners against the proletariat and peasantry.

Dimorphism The state of having two different forms within a single species. Sexual dimorphism (from the Greek *di-*, meaning twice, and *morphe*, meaning form), for example, is the difference – by colour, shape, size or body parts – between male and female members of the same species.

Dispensationalism A doctrine of evangelical Christianity that interprets the Bible as revealing a chronological series of "dispensations" – periods of history in which God revealed himself and his plan for salvation. The doctrine stems from the ideas of John Nelson Darby, an Anglo-Irish preacher who was one of the founders of the Brethren movement of fundamentalist Christianity (see Darbyism). Crucial to dispensationalism is the idea of the millennium, when Christ the Messiah will appear again and establish the kingdom of God on Earth for 1,000 years until the Day of Judgment and the "rapture" – the "catching up" – by which believers will be carried up to heaven. Dispensationalism holds that God will fulfil his promises to Israel, giving Jews the possibility of embracing Christ as the Messiah at his second coming. This idea is one reason for the strong support among America's fundamentalist Christians for the modern state of Israel.

Divisionism Another word for pointillism, the neo-impressionist style of painting (see Impressionism) – practised especially in France by Georges Seurat (1859–91), Camille Pissarro (1830–1903) and his son, Lucien Pissarro (1863–1944) – in which the artist uses tiny dots of pure colour that then merge together in the viewer's eye.

Dixiecratism The ideology, notably a belief in racial segregation, of a group of conservative politicians in the southern states of America who seceded from the mainstream Democratic Party in 1948 in opposition to the party's policy of extending civil rights. The "Dixiecrats" met in July 1948 in Birmingham, Alabama, to nominate Governor Strom Thurmond (1902–2003) of South Carolina as their nominee for president (he won Louisiana, Mississippi, Alabama and South Carolina). The official name of the Dixiecrats' party was the States' Rights Democratic Party, which underlined its desire to maintain the southern way of life against what it saw as federal interference. Though the party disbanded after the 1948 election, Dixiecrat views remained influential in the southern states for decades and ensured that the Democratic Party "lost" the south to a Republican Party less enamoured of progress in civil rights (Thurmond himself switched to the Republican Party). The word "Dixiecrat" is an amalgam of Dixie and Democrat, with Dixie meaning the southern states, especially those of the Confederacy during the American civil war. *Dixie* was the title of a marching song of the Confederate army composed by Daniel Decatur Emmett (1815–1904) in 1859, and the word probably comes from the $10 notes issued before 1860 by a New Orleans bank. The notes, used by French-speaking residents of the city, had the word *dix* – French for ten – printed on them.

Dogmatism The arrogant and stubborn adherence to an opinion or doctrine (*dogma* in Greek), regardless of dissenting fact or opinion.

Donatism A schismatic Christian movement in North Africa, formed in 311 by followers of Donatus Magnus (died c355), a theologian in Carthage in what is now Tunisia. The schism with the rest of Christianity occurred because the Donatists objected to the appointment of a certain Caecilian as bishop of Carthage on the grounds that he had been consecrated by Felix, a bishop who had traitorously surrendered copies of the Scriptures to the Roman authorities during Emperor Diocletian's persecution of the Christians. Fundamental to their stance was the heretical view that only those living a blameless life belonged to the church, and that the validity of the sacrament depended on the personal merit of the priest administering it. Despite periods of persecution, Donatism became the majority sect in North Africa for much of the 4th century, until in the early 5th century it lost ground to the preaching of St Augustine (354–430). In 411 a conference in Carthage presided over by a friend of Augustine, the imperial tribune Marcellinus, decided against the Donatists and in favour of the Catholics. This led to increasing persecution of the Donatists. By the 7th century both Donatism and other forms of Christianity in North Africa had been more or less ended by the Muslim conquest.

Dualism The idea that there are two distinct and coexisting aspects or realities – for example, the spiritual and the material, good and evil, light and darkness. The notion has an impressive heritage, with Plato arguing that there is a physical reality, the world of phenomena, and a world of ideas. Dualism is inherent in much of religion – for example, in the Manichaean notion of a world balanced between the forces of good and evil (see Manichaeism), or in the Taoist notion of yin and yang, symbolising the duality of nature (see Taoism). The idea of a dualism of mind and body was a preoccupation of the French philosopher René Descartes (1596–1650), popularly known for declaring: "*Cogito, ergo sum*" (I think, therefore I am).

Dwarfism The physical state in which a person is excessively small for his or her age. There are more than 200 medical conditions that can cause dwarfism, the most common being achondroplasia, in which the limbs are short in comparison with the torso.

Dystopianism The belief that a situation is extremely bad or unhappy – the opposite of **utopianism**. Dystopian – from the Greek *dys*, meaning bad, and *topos*, meaning place – is an adjective first used by John Stuart Mill (in the British House of Commons in 1868) as the contrary of the imaginary and perfect Utopia described in Thomas More's 1516 book. Dystopianism occurs frequently in literature, for example in Aldous Huxley's *Brave New World* and Ray Bradbury's *Fahrenheit 451*.

e

Eclecticism From the Greek for "choosing" (obviously the best), an approach to life and thought that draws on many sources, rather than relying on only one view or set of assumptions. The term was first employed by Greek philosophers in the 2nd and 1st centuries BC, seeking – in the absence of absolute truth – to reach the highest degree of probability. Among the Romans, Cicero and Seneca were similarly eclectic. In a general sense, eclecticism can be relevant to many human endeavours, from painting to music and even to the martial arts.

Economism A belief in the supremacy of economic factors, so that social factors, such as culture or race, are reduced to their economic dimensions or simply ignored. The term, derived from the Greek *oikonomia*, meaning household management, has its critics. An American social critic, Albert Jay Nock (1873–1945), castigated economism as a philosophy "which interprets the whole sum of human life in terms of the production, acquisition, and distribution of wealth ... I have sometimes thought that here may be the rock on which western civilisation will finally shatter itself". The term was also used as a label for a group of moderate Russian Social Democrats at the end of the 19th century who argued that the concern of the working class should be the improvement of its living conditions rather than political reform.

Egalitarianism The doctrine that all people are or should be equal, enjoying the same political, social and economic rights. The concept, at least as old as the Old Testament, provides the opening lines to America's 1776 Declaration of Independence ("We hold these truths to be self-evident, that all men are created equal ..."), is fundamental to the constitution of the French Republic and is a basic principle of **communism**. Cynics note that so-called egalitarian societies still produce their own elites.

Egocentrism The attitude in which a person considers himself or herself to be at the centre of the universe. Psychologists note that egocentrics cannot properly differentiate themselves from the world around them; they are unable to "put themselves in others' shoes". The Swiss psychologist Jean Piaget (1896–1980) considered this to be normal for children.

Egoism The theory, from the Latin *ego*, meaning I, that the goal of an individual is or should be whatever is in his or her own interest. By contrast, **altruism** considers the interests of others, too.

Egotism The habit of giving oneself an exaggerated sense of self-importance.

Elitism The belief that a select group, or elite, is superior to those outside the group by virtue of this elite's superior characteristics – for example, by bloodline, education or intelligence. America has its Ivy League elite; France its *grandes écoles*; and Britain its Oxbridge elite and "old school tie" network.

Emotionalism A tendency to exhibit emotion, particularly too much emotion.

Empiricism The theory, going back as far as Aristotle (384–322BC), that knowledge comes from experience, or observable evidence – an approach fundamental to science. The term originated in the 19th century, but was basic to the ideas of many philosophers in the 17th and 18th centuries, such as the English John Locke (1632–1704), the Irish George Berkeley (1685–1753) and the Scottish David Hume (1711–76), who preferred the empirical method to the abstractions of metaphysics. The guiding principle of empiricism is summed up in the Latin tag "*nihil in intellectu nisi prius in sensu*" – nothing in the intellect unless first in the sense(s). One problem for empiricism, however, is the difficulty of explaining knowledge – such as in mathematics – that appears to have no basis in experience.

Environmentalism A political and social movement that seeks to protect the natural environment, both flora and fauna, from pollution and other forms of damage. Legislation that can be considered "environmental" can be traced back to the beginnings of the industrial revolution in Europe and America. The Sierra Club in America, established to conserve nature and its resources, was founded as long ago as 1892, but as a mass movement environmentalism is a phenomenon of the latter part of the 20th century. America's Environmental Protection Agency, for example, was created in 1970 amid protests at the harmful use of DDT and America's Endangered Species Act was signed in 1973. Similarly, Greenpeace, originally established to oppose American nuclear tests, was founded in Canada in 1971; Friends of the Earth was founded in America in 1969, becoming an international network in 1971. In the 21st century environmentalism, especially in the West (the movement is much weaker in developing countries), has often been associated with anti-globalism.

Epicureanism The way of life taught by the Greek philosopher Epicurus (c341–270BC), who argued that the goal of life was to be happy, since there was no after-life. This is often construed as "eat, drink and be merry, for tomorrow we die" – but in fact Epicurus did not advocate such a hedonistic approach, since the resulting hangover would mean the very pain that should be avoided. Instead, he emphasised moderation as a way of achieving tranquillity, happiness and freedom from fear.

Episcopalianism The governance of a church by bishops, as opposed to the system of Presbyterianism – governance by elders – or **Congregationalism** (governance by assemblies of believers). The term comes from the Greek *episkopos*, or bishop (*epi skopos* means over sight), and the system was common in early Christianity. After the Reformation in the 16th century, the term referred to Protestant churches not in communion with the Catholic church in Rome, in particular the Church of England (the Anglican church). The Episcopal church is the name borne by the Anglican church in America (where it was established in 1607 and where there are now around 2m Episcopalians) and Scotland. The late 1990s saw divisions in the worldwide Anglican Communion when conservative Anglican bishops from developing countries, especially in Africa, objected to the ordination of practising homosexuals by the Episcopal church in America. The Church of England now ordains women as priests and has agreed to ordain them as bishops; the Episcopal church, in both America and Scotland, already ordains them as bishops.

Essenism The doctrines and practices of the Essenes, a Jewish religious brotherhood that flourished in Palestine, near the Dead Sea, from the 2nd century BC to the end of the 1st century AD. The Essenes lived in ascetic, monastic communities, generally excluding women, and were rigorous in their observance of the Law of Moses contained in the Torah. The Essenes, unlike the contemporary Pharisees, denied the resurrection of the body. They also believed that the Day of Judgment was imminent. The Dead Sea Scrolls, discovered in 1947, are believed to have belonged to the Essenes.

Essentialism The idea that things (or people) have properties and characteristics that define them, and so differentiate them from others – as a human being, for example, is different from a chimpanzee. In philosophy, this leads to distinguishing between features that are essential and those that are accidental (a human being by necessity occupies space – an essential characteristic – and probably wears clothes, which are merely accidental to the person's essence). In education, essentialism is the view that children need to be taught the ideas seen as essential to the national culture.

Ethnocentrism The belief that one's own culture and ethnic group are superior to others – and so a tendency to evaluate other cultures in terms of one's own. Ethnocentrism has been part of human nature through the ages, witness the habit of labelling foreigners and outsiders as "savages" and "barbarians". Sir John Lubbock (1834–1913), a British banker and politician who was also a leading anthropologist of his era, thought all non-literate peoples were without religion; the French anthropologist Lucien Lévy-Bruhl (1857–1939) described "primitive" societies as having a "prelogical mentality" because their world view was unlike that of Europeans. By contrast, Sir Edward Evan Evans-Pritchard (1902–73), a noted British anthropologist, wrote: "This ethnocentric attitude has to be abandoned if we are to appreciate the rich variety of human culture and social life." The first use of the term was probably in 1900 when W.J. McGee (1853–1912), an American anthropologist, referred to ethnocentrism as a characteristic of primitive cultures

– not imagining, it seems, that it could be a characteristic of his own culture, too.

Euphemism An understatement (from the Greek *eu*, meaning well, and *pheme*, meaning speaking), designed to minimise harshness or embarrassment – for example, to "let go" rather than "fire" an employee. Sometimes a euphemism loses its intended purpose: "ethnic cleansing" and "collateral damage" no longer obscure the meaning of racial massacre and civilian casualties.

Euphuism An ornate and affected way of speaking or writing – for example, with an excessive use of alliteration, repetition, similes and antitheses. The word, from the Greek *euphues*, meaning well-endowed by nature or shapely, refers to the protagonist of two books of this style – *Euphues: the Anatomy of Wit* and *Euphues and his England* – by John Lyly (c1554–1606), an English writer, in 1578 and 1580. One extract from *Euphues: the Anatomy of Wit*, is typical of the style: "It is virtue, yea virtue, gentlemen, that maketh gentlemen; that maketh the poor rich, the base-born noble, the subject a sovereign, the deformed beautiful, the sick whole, the weak strong, the most miserable most happy." Euphuism, however, was not Lyly's alone, but was common in the late 16th century, especially in the language of the Elizabethan court.

Eurocommunism A political ideology adopted by some communist parties in western Europe in the 1970s and 1980s that advocated democratic procedures and stressed independence from the Soviet Union. Eurocommunism was developed in particular by the communist parties of Italy, Spain and (less enthusiastically) France, partly in response to the well-publicised human-rights abuses in the Soviet Union and the crushing of dissent in 1968 in what was then Czechoslovakia, and partly to make themselves more relevant to voters. The Italian and Spanish parties agreed in 1975 that the Soviet Union was not the sole model for social and economic change; that all progressive forces should collaborate for "the democratic and socialist renewal of society"; and that communist parties needed to revive themselves by democratising their internal organisation. The French communist party agreed to this "new way" in 1977, but in the 1980s reverted to the pro-Soviet line. With the collapse of the Soviet Union at the start of the 1990s, support for communism in Europe – including for Eurocommunism – fell into insignificance.

Evangelicalism A movement in Protestant Christianity that emphasises the experience of conversion, the Bible as the sole basis of faith and the importance of evangelism. The movement began in Europe and America in the mid-18th century, with men such as George Whitefield (1714–70), a British evangelist whose preaching in America led to the religious revival known in Britain's American colonies as the Great Awakening. Later, it attracted the support of the British politician and anti-slavery campaigner William Wilberforce (1759–1833). Evangelicalism has remained an especially strong social, and indeed political, force in America, with the revivalist fervour of the 19th century turning, thanks to preachers such as Billy Graham, Jerry Falwell and Pat Robertson, into the **fundamentalism** and **Pentecostalism** of the 20th and now 21st centuries.

Evangelism The mission to convert people to a religion, in particular to Christianity or Islam, both of which have a scriptural duty to spread the word of God. The term originates in the Greek *euangelos*, meaning "bringing good news". In a more general sense, evangelism can be the enthusiastic advocacy of a cause (for example, environmental evangelism).

Exhibitionism Behaviour deliberately intended to draw attention to oneself. As defined by psychiatrists, exhibitionism is the compulsion to expose one's genitals in public or to someone not expecting the exposure. It can also include the compulsion to have sexual intercourse in circumstances where one might be seen.

Existentialism A philosophical approach in which individuals are seen as free agents, determining their development through acts of will. Existentialism began with the work of Kierkegaard and Nietzsche in the 19th century, but the term was probably coined by a French philosopher, Gabriel Marcel (1889–1973), in 1943, and the approach is most closely associated with the 20th-century French philosophers Jean-Paul Sartre (1905–80) and Albert Camus (1913–60). Sartre published *L'Etre et le Néant* (Being and Nothingness) in 1943; Camus published *Le Mythe de Sisyphe* (The Myth of Sisyphus) in 1942, illustrating the futility of existence. Fundamental to existentialism is the notion that existence comes before essence, meaning that the actual life of an individual is what constitutes his essence, instead of a predetermined essence defining the human being. Existentialism tends to deny the existence of objective values, emphasising instead a person's freedom and experience.

Exorcism The expulsion of an evil spirit from a person or place. The practice goes back for millennia, and is recognised in the New Testament as one of Christ's miracles. Exorcism is a rite of Christianity but most denominations, especially in the West, now use it sparingly. By contrast, Scientologists believe that every person is possessed by alien beings known as "body thetans", who must be exorcised by Scientology's own techniques.

Expansionism A policy of gaining more territory or greater markets and economic influence. The process is often associated with colonialism.

Expressionism A movement in the arts, particularly painting, in which the artist stresses subjective or emotional feelings above purely objective observations. The movement had its roots in the late 19th century but was defined in Germany at the start of the 20th century by artists such as Max Beckmann (1884–1950) and soon spread throughout Europe, embracing painters as varied as the Norwegian Edvard Munch (1863–1944) and the Russian émigré in France Marc Chagall (1887–1985).

Extremism The quality, invariably negative, of going beyond
normally accepted practices, especially in politics. The
contrast is with moderation. An extremist might well
assassinate a political opponent; a moderate would not.
Not enjoying the label, an extremist might well prefer to
be called a radical.

f

Fabianism The doctrine of the Fabian Society, founded in London in 1884 with the goal of achieving socialism through evolutionary steps. Its aim, in its own words, was "the reconstruction of Society in accordance with the highest moral principles", but only gradually rather than through the revolution advocated by Marxism. The name is an allusion to the Roman general Quintus Fabius Maximus, whose nickname was *Cunctator* – the delayer. Fabianism, whose early luminaries included Sidney and Beatrice Webb (1859–1947 and 1858–1943) and George Bernard Shaw (1856–1950), was extremely influential in the British Labour Party, which sprang from the efforts of the early Fabians. It also influenced several leaders of the 20th-century independence movements in Britain's colonies, notably in India, where Jawaharlal Nehru (1889–1964), India's first prime minister, devised the country's economic policy on Fabian lines. The founder of Pakistan, Muhammad Ali Jinnah (1876–1948), had been a Fabian in the 1930s; and independent Singapore's first prime minister, Lee Kuan Yew, was also for a time influenced by Fabianism.

Factionalism The state of having divisions, for example in a
political movement. Factions are normally considered to
be bad, since they militate against cohesion and unity.

Falangism Specifically, the fascist doctrine of the Spanish
Falange Party, which was founded in 1933 by José
António Primo de Rivera and supported General Franco
in the Spanish civil war of 1936–39 (Falange means a
phalanx formation, from the Greek for battalion). More
generally, the term applies to the fascist doctrines of
several right-wing political organisations, especially in
Latin America from the 1930s onwards (see fascism).
When spelled Phalangism, it refers to the programme of
the Christian Lebanese Kataeb (or Phalange) Party, which
led the Christian forces in the Lebanese civil war of
1975–90.

Fanaticism The exhibition of excessive and obsessive zeal,
common among followers of sport, religion and politics.
The difference between a fan and a fanatic is that a fan
behaves in an acceptable way; a fanatic, by going to
excess, does not.

Fascism An authoritarian system of government,
characterised by nationalism. The word derives from the
Latin *fasces*, or bundle, with the symbol of a bound
bundle of sticks and a protruding axe-blade indicating
collective power in ancient Rome. The word was first
used for the dictatorial regime of Benito Mussolini
(1883–1945) in Italy from 1922 to 1943, and for the ideology
in the 1930s and later of Franco in Spain and Hitler in

Germany. In economic terms, fascism opposes both
Marxism, with its class warfare, and individual **capitalism**,
favouring instead what Mussolini called "the corporate
state", with government control – not least with business
cartels – over the economy. In political terms, fascism
exalts the nation and racial purity: a people must be
strong to survive in competition with other races.
Following the horrors of the second world war, the term
is now invariably pejorative, frequently applied to
right-wing governments in Latin America (for example,
Chile under General Pinochet) and to extremist
nationalist and anti-immigrant movements in Europe.

Fatalism The belief that everything is predetermined, and so
inevitable. The implication is that free will does not exist.
Religion is sometimes associated with fatalism, because
of the argument that "it is God's will".

Fauvism A style of painting that flourished briefly in France at
the beginning of the 20th century. The Fauvists, led by
Henri Matisse (1869–1954), used pure, brilliant colours
applied directly on to the canvas in an explosion of
colour. Their first formal exhibition was in 1905 at the
annual Paris *Salon d'Automne*, where the critic Louis
Vauxcelles (1870–1945) described Matisse's painting *Open
Window and Woman with the Hat* as "*Donatello au milieu
des fauves*" (Donatello among the wild beasts – *fauve*
means wild animal). Other Fauvists were Georges Braque
(1882–1963), André Derain (1880–1954), Raoul Dufy
(1877–1953) and Maurice de Vlaminck (1876–1958). Fauvism
was initially greeted with shock by the artistic elite, but

was immediately embraced by the American collector Gertrude Stein (1874–1946). Even so, the style more or less died out after 1908 as most of the Fauvists turned away from their vivid expressionism to the geometrical style of cubism (so named in 1908 by the same Louis Vauxcelles).

Favouritism The practice of giving preference, often undeserved, to one person or group at the expense of another. Sometimes this can be government policy, as in Malaysia, with economic preference for the Malays – the *bumiputra*, or "sons of the soil" – at the expense of their ethnic Chinese and Indian compatriots.

Federalism A system of government, as in the United States, in which power is shared between a national authority (the federal government in America) and political units such as states or provinces. Federalism has been adopted in many parts of the world, from India and Australia to Brazil and Belgium. The concept, however, has proved controversial in the evolution of the European Union, with Eurosceptics, especially in Britain, claiming that the EU is on the way to becoming a federal "United States of Europe".

Feminism A movement arguing that women should have equal rights to men in all spheres of life. Feminism goes back at least to the 18th century, with the writings, for example, of Mary Wollstonecraft (1759–97), but became prominent in the struggle for voting rights at the turn of the 19th and 20th centuries (New Zealand women gained the vote in 1893; British women in 1918; American women in 1919; French women not until 1944). Although Simone de Beauvoir (1908–86) wrote the influential book *The Second Sex* in 1949, modern feminism is essentially a development from the 1960s, when the term "Women's Liberation" was coined in America and feminist writers such as Betty Friedan (1921–2006), Angela Davis and Gloria Steinem became prominent. In the 21st century feminism has in theory largely achieved its goals in the developed world, not least by legislation. In practice, women in general still earn less than men and are less represented in senior positions. In some developing countries – for example, Afghanistan and Pakistan – conditions for women seem to have worsened.

Fenianism   A revolutionary movement, with the Fenian Brotherhood founded in America in 1858, that sought the independence of Ireland from Britain. The Fenians mounted an abortive revolt in Ireland in 1867 and continued their armed struggle into the early 20th century, after which they were succeeded by the Irish Republican Army (IRA). Fenianism (derived from the Old Irish *féne*, the name of an ancient Irish people) gained much of its support from Irish Americans, some of whom made unsuccessful raids into British-ruled Canada in the late 19th century.

Fetishism   The worship of an inanimate object for its supposed magical power. The word originated in the 17th century from the French *fétiche* and Portuguese *feitiço*, meaning amulet or charm, used in connection with the customs of West Africa. In psychology, borrowing the term from anthropology, fetishism is a mental condition in which the use of a non-genital, asexual object – such as a shoe or foot – is necessary to achieve sexual gratification. Sigmund Freud, in his *Three Contributions to the Theory of Sex*, described the object of the fetishist as comparable to "the fetich in which the savage sees the embodiment of his god".

Feudalism   The political and social system that prevailed in much of medieval Europe, in which the monarch would grant land (a "feud" or fief) to noblemen (called barons in Britain), who would then lease the land to knights. The knights would in turn lease the land to villeins or serfs. This chain created a reciprocal chain of obligation: the serfs would provide food and service to the knights, who would provide military protection to the barons, who would provide an army and money for the monarch. The term "feudalism" was not used until the 17th century, by which time it was already losing prominence owing to the growth of urban settlements. In a rather loose sense feudalism still exists in many developing countries, where peasants give their loyalty (and part of their crops) to a land-owning ruling class that in return provides them with protection (such as housing or even education).

Fordism   The concept of mass production and mass consumption developed by Henry Ford (1863–1947), founder of the Ford Motor Company, in the early 20th century. Because higher production could be justified only by higher consumption, Fordism – a term seemingly coined in the 1930s by Antonio Gramsci (1891–1937), an

Italian Marxist – also required wages high enough for consumers to buy the products. One implication of Fordism is corporate **paternalism**, with the employer providing benefits, such as health insurance, for the workers.

Formalism The theory, in art, literature, ethics and even mathematics, that what matters is adherence to already known forms. In painting, for example, formalism, reacting to **Impressionism**, argued that a painting – no matter what its subject – was "essentially a flat surface covered in colours arranged in a certain order", in the words of Maurice Denis (1870–1943), a French artist and designer. As such, formalism prepared the way for abstract art. In literary analysis, formalism concentrates on the text itself, rather than its historical or cultural context.

Fourierism A philosophy of social reform proposed by the French social theorist Charles Fourier (1772–1837), who envisaged the reorganisation of society into self-sufficient, independent co-operatives known as phalanxes (*phalanges* in French). The idea was one of several utopian schemes in the early 19th century, and was transplanted, under the name "Associationism", by Albert Brisbane (1809–90) to America, where it was publicised by the *New York Tribune* newspaper. Fourier's theory was that people in his co-operatives would live a life of harmony, free from government interference. In America around 50 phalanxes – forerunners of the hippy communes of the late 20th century – were established, with members paid according to the unpleasantness of their work. However, the average lifespan of the phalanxes was a mere two years.

Francoism The ideology of General Francisco Franco (1892–1975), victorious leader of the Nationalist forces in the 1936–39 Spanish civil war and dictator of Spain until his death in 1975. Franco sided with the fascist regimes of Italy and Germany in the 1930s but kept Spain neutral during the second world war and sided with America in the subsequent "cold war". Francoism's characteristics were essentially authoritarianism, nationalism, anti-communism and an adherence to Roman Catholicism.

Freudianism The psychological theories of the Austrian neurologist Sigmund Freud (1856–1939), who stressed the importance of unconscious feelings and sexuality in determining a person's actions and beliefs. Freudianism teaches the dynamic interaction between the id, the ego and the superego, representing respectively a person's instinct, will and moral conscience.

Frotteurism The technique in art of taking a rubbing from an uneven surface. Also know as *frottage* (French for rubbing), the technique was used by Max Ernst (1891–1976) and other members of the surrealist movement as a starting point for their compositions (see surrealism). In psychology, frotteurism is the practice of achieving sexual pleasure by rubbing against the clothing of another person.

Fundamentalism A belief in a basic set of rules or doctrinal teachings, especially in religion – notably, in the 20th and 21st centuries, those of Christianity and Islam. Fundamentalist Christians, for example, believe in a literal interpretation of the Bible, including its account of the creation of the world and of Christ's miracles. Fundamentalist Muslims believe that the Koran is God's word and advocate the application of *sharia* Islamic law. The term is often used pejoratively, linking fundamentalism to extremism.

Futurism A movement in art and literature launched by an Italian poet, Filippo Tommaso Marinetti (1876-1944), with the publication in 1909 of the Manifesto of Futurism in *La Gazzetta dell'Emilia* and then on the front page of the French newspaper *Le Figaro*. The idea was to reject all previous schools of art and to see the world as one of movement and mechanised dynamism (the manifesto, for example, exalted the power and speed of the motor car). Prominent futurist painters included Umberto Boccioni (1882-1916), Giacomo Balla (1871-1958) and Gino Severini (1883-1966). Futurism saw war as a cleansing experience, and many Italian futurists were quick to identify with the fascism of Benito Mussolini.

g

Gallicanism A political and ecclesiastical doctrine in France asserting the freedom of French Roman Catholics from the absolute authority of the pope. The word was coined in the 19th century to describe opposition to the concept of ultramontanism (which asserted the power over Catholics in France of the pope "beyond the mountains" in Italy). But as a doctrine its roots lie in early French nationalism, in the 8th and 9th centuries, and then in the conflict between Philip IV (1268–1314), known as "the Fair", and Pope Boniface VIII (c1235–1303 and pope 1294–1303), when the king levied a 50% tax on the clergy. After later conflicts between kings and popes, Charles VII in 1438 issued the Pragmatic Sanction of Bourges, giving the French church authority to control its own appointments and administration independent of the pope. By the end of the 16th century two strands of Gallicanism had evolved: political (both parliamentary and royal) and theological. The Four Gallican Articles, approved by the French clergy in 1682, combined both strands: the pope had supreme spiritual authority but no secular power; the pope was subject to ecumenical councils; the pope must accept the customs of the French church, such as the right of the monarch to appoint bishops; and papal infallibility is conditional on approval by the whole church. Royal Gallicanism became irrelevant after the fall of the monarchy and theological Gallicanism ended when the First Vatican Council in 1869–70 declared the pope infallible in matters of faith and morals and confirmed the doctrine of ultramontanism.

Gallicism An expression or idiom in the French language, particularly when used by speakers of a different language – for example, *savoir faire* or *joie de vivre.*

Gaullism The policies of conservatism and French nationalism – characterised in particular by a refusal to be dependent on America – developed by Charles de Gaulle (1890–1970), both as a leader of the Free French in the second world war and as president of France during the 1960s. One decision by de Gaulle was that France should possess an independent nuclear deterrent; a second was to withdraw from the military arm of NATO (a decision reversed in 2009 by President Nicolas Sarkozy). Gaullism has survived de Gaulle's death in 1970, being a strong current in both centre and centre-right politics in France, initially with the centrist Union of Democrats for the Republic and the more right-wing Rally for the Republic (RPR). Gaullism is now represented mainly by Sarkozy's Union for a Popular Movement (UMP), the successor to the RPR.

Geocentrism The belief that the Earth is the centre of the universe. Science has long since disproved this (Copernicus and Galileo put the sun at the centre of our solar system as long ago as the 16th and 17th centuries – see **heliocentrism**), but it remains a tenet of many Christian fundamentalists and creationists (see **fundamentalism** and **creationism**).

Geophagism The practice, also known as geophagy (from the Greek *geo*, meaning earth, and *phagia*, meaning eating), of eating clay or other earth. The practice has been observed in most parts of the world, particularly in Africa and among native Americans and historically among slaves in America. The nutritional justification is the presence of minerals in the earth.

Germanism A loan word from the German language for use in another language – for example, kindergarten.

Gigantism The condition, often caused by a hormonal imbalance, of being excessively tall.

Globalism A belief in **internationalism**, particularly in terms of institutions and organisations such as the United Nations, in contrast to the narrower practices of **nationalism** and **regionalism**.

Gnosticism A heresy popular in 2nd-century Christianity that taught that the world was created by the demiurge – a heavenly being subordinate to the supreme being. Christ was supposedly sent by this supreme being, and esoteric knowledge (*gnosis* in Greek) of this supreme being would redeem the human spirit. Gnosticism distinguished between this supreme divinity and the demiurge. The demiurge was the imperfect creator and ruler of a world that was itself imperfect. Some individuals, however, might hope to return to the supreme being after death, with Christ having acted as a redeemer (with perhaps other redeemers to follow) and bringing *gnosis* with him. Some Gnostics held that human beings are classified by flesh, soul and spirit (the divine spark). The purely corporeal could never be saved; those possessed knowingly of the divine spark could look forward to certain salvation; and those in between might attain a lesser salvation through faith. Though Gnosticism is identified with Christianity, its dualistic nature, dividing the world into two entities, is common to many other beliefs, such as Manichaeism, including some, such as Zoroastrianism, which pre-date Christianity.

Goldwynism   A comical phrase resulting from a contradictory choice of words, idiom or context, as in "include me out". The term refers to an habitual user of such phrases, namely Samuel Goldwyn (1882–1974), a Polish-born American film producer, who was born Schmuel Gelfisz but changed his name to Samuel Goldfish in Britain and then, in America, to Samuel Goldwyn. Well-known examples of Goldwynisms include: "If I could drop dead right now, I'd be the happiest man alive" and "I may not always be right, but I'm never wrong."

Gradualism In politics, the policy of gradual reform rather
    than abrupt change or revolution. As such, gradualism
    tends to be a feature of conservatism. In science,
    gradualism is the notion that evolution proceeds by
    incremental changes.

h

Hasidism A mystical Jewish movement founded in Poland in the 18th century as a reaction against rigid Talmudic worship and offering in its stead joyful worship through music and dance. The movement, from the Hebrew *hasid*, meaning pious one, began with the preaching of Israel ben Eliezer Ba'Al Shem Tov (1698–1760), known by the acronym Besht, who taught that God was immanent in all things and that piety was more important than scholarship. The Hasidim were excommunicated by the Talmudists of Orthodox Judaism in 1772 but continued to grow in popularity in central and eastern Europe. By the 19th century the Hasidim had become ultra-conservative and been accepted again by the Orthodox. By the late 20th century they had become the staunchest opponents of secularism in Jewish life. The Hasidim, recognisable by clothing such as broad-brimmed fur hats, which originated with 18th-century Polish nobility, suffered horrendously during the Holocaust in Europe; today, they are concentrated in Israel and America, where the largest community is the Lubavitch group, with perhaps 100,000 followers. The term Hasidim has also been applied to a strictly observant Jewish sect that developed between 300BC and 175BC and led the opposition to the Hellenising campaign of Antiochus IV (c215–164BC) of Syria. A further use of the word Hasidism refers to a movement in Germany in the 12th and 13th centuries that combined asceticism with Kabbalistic mysticism.

Hedonism The pursuit of pleasure and the practice of self-indulgence – and therefore doubtless as old as mankind, though the term itself (from the Greek *hedone*, meaning pleasure) originated in the mid-19th century. Hedonists are in modern times frequently characterised as selfish seekers of their own pleasure, but in classical Greece the concept of hedonism was more usually associated with tranquillity and intellectual joy rather than with the pleasures of the flesh. An exception, with a preference for sensuality, was Aristippus (c435–356BC). More typical, though, was Epicurus (341–270BC), who argued that tranquillity came from wisdom and virtue.

Heightism Discrimination on the basis of a person's height, normally favouring the tall over the short. Although there are plenty of obvious exceptions, from Napoleon to Deng Xiaoping and now President Nicolas Sarkozy of France, sociological surveys constantly assert that tall people do better in business, politics and love.

Heliocentrism The theory, elaborated by the Polish astronomer Nicolaus Copernicus (1473–1543) in the 16th century (though the idea had been toyed with by astronomers for centuries before), that the sun is the centre of the universe. This was at odds with the geocentric view of the Roman Catholic church (see geocentrism), which in 1633 famously found Italy's Galileo Galilei (1564–1642) guilty of heresy for his support of the Copernican thesis.

Hellenism The culture and civilisation of Greece, especially ancient Greece (from the Greek root *Hellas*, meaning Greece). The word refers also to the assimilation of Greek customs and language, for example by Jews from the 4th century BC to the 1st century AD, a period in which Hellenic influence dominated the Middle East and Mediterranean.

Henotheism Adherence to one particular god out of several. The word, from the Greek *heno-*, meaning one, and *theos*, meaning god, was coined by Max Müller (1823–1900), a German philologist and orientalist, to describe situations in which someone might decide to worship one god from the pantheon of gods. Henotheism is similar to monolatry, but whereas henotheism does not preclude the existence of other gods worthy of worship, monolatry holds that only one god is worthy – even though others are known to exist.

Hermaphroditism (or hermaphrodism) The condition of having both male and female sexual characteristics. In many plants and invertebrates the condition is common (a flower, for example, may have both stamens and pistils); in humans it is rare and is almost always confined to appearance rather than function.

Hermeticism In literature, hermeticism (*ermetismo* in Italian)
was a modernist poetry movement in Italy in the early
20th century. The movement's poets, notably Giuseppe
Ungaretti (1888–1970), Salvatore Quasimodo (1901–68)
and Eugenio Montale (1896–1981) – the last two both
Nobel laureates – drew their influence from 19th-century
French symbolist poets (see **symbolism**), such as Charles
Baudelaire (1821–67) and Arthur Rimbaud (1854–91), and
also from **futurism**, a short-lived Italian movement that
encouraged innovation in language. In philosophy,
hermeticism refers both to a 1st-century AD form of
neoplatonism, marrying rationality with religion, centred
on Alexandria and to a set of beliefs encompassing the
occult, alchemy and astrology (the derivation is from the
Greek god Hermes, who is identified with the Egyptian
Thoth, regarded as the founder of alchemy and
astrology).

Heroism Great bravery. Oddly, this is not always true of
heroes (or heroines), who may simply be the protagonists
of a book or film. Similarly devaluing the concept is the
tendency to describe victims of war or **terrorism** as
"heroes", regardless of any action, brave or not, on their
part.

Hinduism A religious and cultural tradition, dominant in
India, which can claim to be the world's oldest faith, with
some authorities setting its origins around 4000BC, and
which, with around 900m followers, is the world's third
most popular, after Christianity and Islam. Hinduism's
primary texts are the *Vedas*, summarised in the Bhagavad

Gita, featuring Krishna, regarded by Hindus as the supreme manifestation of God. Hinduism is often considered polytheistic (see **polytheism**), but most strands of the religion recognise a single supreme deity, with various gods and goddesses being simply manifestations of that supreme God. Because divinity is in every being, Hinduism promotes non-violence and, for most followers, **vegetarianism**. Crucial to the religion is a belief in reincarnation, decided by the law of karma (the effect of one's actions), and ended only by the salvation (*moksha* or nirvana) gained by the attainment of perfect peace. Also embedded in Hindu society (though some authorities say not in the texts) is the concept of caste, with society being divided into four principal classes: the Brahmins, or priests; the Kshatriyas, or warriors and nobles; the Vaishyas, or farmers and businessmen; and the Shudras, or servants and labourers.

Historical materialism See dialectical materialism.

Historicism The theory, partly developed by the German philosopher Georg Hegel (1770–1831), that social phenomena are the consequence of history and so can be understood only by understanding historical events, conditions and context, including the tendency for human actions to react against what has gone before (as in **Marxism**'s "thesis, antithesis and synthesis"). The contrast is with the reductionist theory that posits the influence of fundamental principles (see **reductionism**).

Holism The philosophical theory that the parts of a whole cannot be understood without reference to the whole. The term, from the Greek *holos*, meaning whole, was coined by the South African statesman and soldier Jan Smuts (1870–1950), who in a 1926 book noted "the tendency in nature to form wholes, that are greater than the sum of the parts, through creative evolution". But the idea goes back at least as far as Aristotle (384–322BC), who declared: "The whole is more than the sum of its parts." Holism has become important in modern medicine, with the holistic approach being to consider mental and social factors in a patient, as well as simply physical symptoms.

Hooliganism Unruly, anti-social and often violent behaviour, particularly common among soccer fans. The word's origins are in the late 19th century, perhaps linked to Hooligan, a fictional Irish family in a popular song, or perhaps to an 1899 book, *The Hooligan Nights*, by Clarence Rook (1863–1915), a chronicler of working-class London.

Humanism A philosophy, or set of beliefs, that holds that human beings achieve a system of morality through their own reasoning rather than through a belief in any divine being. Humanists are therefore often either atheists or agnostics (see **atheism** and **agnosticism**). The term, as in Renaissance Humanism, can also refer to the cultural movement in Europe in the Middle Ages and the Renaissance that revived the language and learning of classical Greece and Rome (hence "the humanities", as a field of scholarly study).

Humanitarianism A view that all people are human beings, leading to a concern for human welfare, practised in particular by non-governmental agencies such as the Red Cross.

Hypnotism The practice of inducing hypnosis (a word coined in 1842 by James Braid (1795–1860), a Scottish surgeon, from the Greek *hupnos*, or "sleep"), in which a person enters an altered state of consciousness similar to sleep. Braid was the first to use the term hypnotism for this practice rather than mesmerism or animal magnetism.

Hypopituitarism A medical condition characterised by the decreased secretion of hormones by the pituitary gland. The consequence is dwarfism in children and premature ageing in adults.

i

Idealism The practice of having ideals, or ideas of perfection, truth, goodness and other virtues. Not surprisingly, idealists are often thought to be out of touch with reality and idealism is often contrasted with materialism. In terms of philosophy, idealism goes back to Plato (c428–347BC), who regarded the visible world as simply a copy of an ideal world beyond our normal senses.

Ignosticism The attitude, also known as igtheism, that the question of God's existence is meaningless, and so is arguing about it, since definitions of God cannot be proven to be either true or false. The term "ignosticism" was coined in the 1960s by Sherwin Wine (1928–2007), a humanistic rabbi; "igtheism" was coined by Paul Kurtz, a secular humanist, in a 1992 book *The New Skepticism*.

Imagism A movement in early 20th-century British and American poetry, defined around 1912 by a group led by the expatriate American Ezra Pound (1885–1972) and including his former fiancée Hilda Doolittle (1886–1961) and her future husband Richard Aldington (1892–1962).

Based in London, the group took its inspiration from T.E. Hulme (1883–1917), a British writer and former student of mathematics, who was critical of what he saw as the sentimentality and **optimism** of the prevailing Romantic and Victorian poetry. In contrast, the Imagists wrote succinct verse with crisp, clear language. In 1914 Pound turned to **Vorticism**, leaving Amy Lowell (1874–1925) to lead the group. Though the movement was short-lived, Imagism had a lasting effect on British and American poetry, influencing not just T.S. Eliot (1888–1965) and D.H. Lawrence (1885–1930) but also the later Beat generation of poets such as Allen Ginsberg (1926–97).

Imperialism The policy of creating an empire, extending a country's power by conquest, violent or otherwise, diplomacy or trade. Imperialism has been a feature of mankind for millennia, from the Assyrians in the 20th century BC to the British and other European powers and Japan in the "Age of Imperialism" of the 19th century and early 20th century. The process of decolonisation in the second half of the 20th century has virtually ended military imperialism, to be replaced, say cynics, by economic and cultural imperialism.

Impressionism A style of painting, originating in France in the late 1860s, which emphasises the visual effect of the moment, giving light and colour precedence over linear precision. The word was originally a critical reference to Claude Monet's 1872 painting *Impression: Soleil levant* (Impression: Sunrise). Other prominent Impressionists were Pierre-Auguste Renoir (1841–1919), Camille Pissarro

(1830–1903), Alfred Sisley (1839–99) and Paul Cézanne
(1839–1906). The term "Impressionism" can also be
applied to literature and music, where feeling and
impression are more important than accuracy and
structure. Though the definition is vague when applied to
literature and music, the French poets Charles Baudelaire
(1821–67), Arthur Rimbaud (1854–91), Stéphane Mallarmé
(1842–98) and Paul Verlaine (1844–96) have all been
considered Impressionist writers, though more
commonly described as symbolists (see **symbolism**); in
music Maurice Ravel (1875–1937) and Claude Debussy
(1862–1918) have been called Impressionists, though
Debussy said the description was an invention of music
critics.

Individualism An emphasis on being self-reliant and
independent, so favouring individual freedom over
collective control. Individualism is sometimes viewed as
being politically incompatible with **socialism**, hence the
common assumption that capitalist America is the
world's most individualistic nation (see **capitalism**).

Intellectualism The exercise of the intellect – or rational
thought – rather than the emotions. Somewhat
irrationally, intellectuals are often derided in Anglo-
American society, witness the phrase "too clever by half".
By contrast, "the intellectual", for example Jean-Paul
Sartre (1905–80) in the past or Bernard-Henri Lévy today,
is revered in France.

Intentionalism The theory in literary criticism that a literary work should be judged in terms of the intentions of the author. In philosophy the term, from the Latin *intentio*, meaning mental effort or purpose, refers to the idea that consciousness is always consciousness of a physical entity or some aspect of reality – meaning that "pure consciousness" does not exist.

Internationalism The doctrine that favours collaboration and co-operation between nations, usually by promoting international institutions such as the UN.

Interpretivism An approach in anthropology, originating with the work of the German-born American anthropologist Franz Boas (1858–1942), that says that cultures can best be understood through studying how people think and what they think about.

Interventionism Getting involved in the affairs of others – frequently the habit of great powers towards other countries. The term is also used when the state involves itself in business and industry. An example of interventionism in foreign policy was the NATO bombardment of Serbia in 1999. A recent example of interventionism in business was the bailing-out of banks in America, Britain and elsewhere in the global financial crisis of 2008–09.

Irredentism The desire to restore to a country a territory previously belonging to it. The term comes from the Italian *irredenta*, as in *Italia irredenta*, meaning unredeemed Italy, referring to the campaign in the late 19th century and early 20th century for the unification of Italian-speaking lands by wresting from foreign rule areas such as Trentino (which was still part of the Austrian empire after the 1860–70 unification of Italy). Modern examples of irredentism include Spain's claim to the British territory of Gibraltar, Morocco's claim to the Spanish enclaves of Ceuta and Melilla and Afghanistan's claim to Pashtun areas of Pakistan.

Islamism A term, frequently used in a pejorative sense (especially by non-Muslims linking Islamism with terrorism), that defines Islam as a religion that applies to all parts of social, legal and political life. Historically, Islamism was simply an 18th-century French term for Islam; it acquired its modern English sense of Islamic fundamentalism in the 1980s as some Muslims, inspired by the Wahhabite doctrine of Saudi Arabia (see Wahhabism) and by the Islamic revolution in Iran, argued that an apolitical Islam was contrary to the teachings of the Prophet. This anti-secular argument of the Islamists was not, in itself, so new in the 20th century: in Egypt, for example, the Muslim Brotherhood was founded in 1928 under the slogan "the Koran is our constitution".

Isolationism The policy of staying aloof from the concerns of other countries – a non-interventionism often accompanied by economic protectionism. The most obvious example in the modern world is North Korea, but cases of isolationism can be seen throughout history, most notably China from the late 14th century to the first half of the 20th century and Japan from the mid-17th century until Commodore Matthew Perry (1794–1858) sailed into Japan's Edo (Tokyo) Bay in 1853 to force open the trade barriers (a treaty with America was signed the following year). Despite its status as a great power, the United States pursued a policy of non-intervention between the first and second world wars, and isolationism remains popular with many Americans, both Republican and Democratic, who instinctively feel that their country does not need the rest of the world or the interference of international institutions such as the UN or the International Criminal Court.

Isomorphism Having the same or similar form (from the Greek *iso*, meaning equal, and *morphe*, meaning form), so that in biology, for example, two **organisms** of different ancestry can be similar, or, in mathematics, if two objects are isomorphic then any property observed in one will also be true of the other.

j

Jacksonianism The political philosophy of Andrew Jackson (1767–1845), seventh president of America from 1829 to 1837, characterised by a laissez-faire approach to the economy and a desire to spread popular democracy while strengthening the presidency at the expense of Congress.

Jacobinism The political ideology of the Jacobins, a ruthless political group – known as the Club des Jacobins and the Société des Amis de la Constitution – formed, originally by Breton politicians, in 1789 in the immediate aftermath of the French Revolution. The aim was to safeguard the gains of the revolution against any reaction from the aristocrats, but the club split in 1791 over a petition calling for the removal of Louis XVI, with less extreme members forming the rival Feuillants club. At this point leadership of the club was assumed by Maximilien Robespierre (1758–94), who instituted the "Reign of Terror" in which the Jacobins, having crushed the more moderate Girondins, slaughtered thousands of supposed enemies of the revolution. The revolutionary Jacobins were so named because they met in a former monastery in Paris of the Dominican friars, who were called Jacobins after the nearby church of St Jacques. The fall of Robespierre in 1794 meant the fall of the Jacobin club, too, though its spirit was revived in the revolution of 1848 and the Paris Commune of 1871. The influence of Jacobinism (and fear of the excesses of the French Revolution) meant that the term was also used in contemporary Britain to criticise radical reformers.

Jainism An ancient Indian religion, with around 4m followers, which preaches non-violence for any and all forms of living beings – all of which possess souls. Jainism has no supreme divinity or gods or spiritual beings to help believers achieve liberation of the soul from the cycle of birth, death and rebirth. Liberation of the soul occurs by getting rid of karma, the substance that sticks to the soul as a result of a person's behaviour. Virtuous behaviour attracts no karma. The present form of Jainism dates back to the revelations of Mahavira, born Prince Vardhamana in 599BC and supposedly the faith's 24th and last *tirthankar*, a perfectly enlightened being who shows the way to enlightenment. The religion's roots go back about three centuries earlier – and its believers say it has existed since eternity, with neither beginning nor end. Fundamental to the practice of Jainism is to commit no harm: the guiding principles are right belief, right knowledge and right conduct. Non-violence is one of five vows, the others being the avoidance of lying, stealing, sex (celibacy is the ideal) and material possessions.

Jansenism The views of a Flemish theologian, Cornelius Otto
Jansen (1585–1638), who as bishop of Ypres in Belgium
emphasised predestination and maintained that man's
nature was instinctively to choose evil rather than good.
Jansen's denial of free will and his concept of original sin
were influenced by the 4th-century writings of St
Augustine, but the Jansenists' views were judged heretical
in 1653 and 1656 by successive Roman Catholic popes,
who considered them too close to **Calvinism**. In the 18th
century the Jansenists, considered a threat to national
unity in France by Louis XIV, moved their church to
Utrecht in Holland, where it remains today.

Jihadism The practice of *jihad*, meaning striving or struggle in
Arabic, which is a religious duty for every Muslim. *Jihad*,
for most Muslims, is the kind of peaceful struggle against
sin that is common to Christianity and **Judaism**, but the
conventional translation for western usage is "holy war",
with an emphasis on violence. From that comes the
connection of the term, from the late 20th century
onwards, with Islamist war – as in the war of the
mujahideen (those who wage *jihad*) against Soviet troops
in Afghanistan in the 1980s – and Islamist terrorism, as in
the activities in the 21st century of al-Qaeda. The French
scholar Gilles Kepel has coined the term "Salafist-
jihadism" to describe the doctrines of al-Qaeda and the
now-defunct Armed Islamic Group (Groupe Islamique
Armé) in Algeria. (Salafist comes from the Arabic *salaf*,
meaning ancestor or forefather, and therefore hearkens
back to a time when Islam had not supposedly strayed
from its original purity – see **Salafism**.)

Jingoism Extreme **patriotism**, often demonstrated by support for an aggressive foreign policy. The word originated from the phrase "by Jingo" – a euphemism for "by Jesus" – in a British music-hall song of the late 1870s threatening war with Russia (which in 1878 was menacing Constantinople in the Russo-Turkish war). The song's chorus went:

> *We don't want to fight but by jingo if we do,*
> *We've got the ships, we've got the men, and got the money too!*
> *We've fought the Bear before, and while we're Britons true,*
> *The Russians shall not have Constantinople.*

The term "jingoism" was coined by a British radical, George Holyoake (1817–1906), in a letter to the *Daily News* on March 13th 1978.

Journalism The profession (some practitioners would call it a craft or trade) of relaying information, in news reports, opinion columns and editorials, to the public through various media – traditionally newspapers, wire services, radio and television but now increasingly the internet. Journalism, which began in 18th-century Europe with the advent of mechanised printing, is often called "the Fourth Estate", the other three being the nobility, clergy and commoners, which were recognised as society's basic divisions in medieval Europe. In democracies, journalists play a vital role in calling governments and any and all parts of the establishment to account – despite which, they are often held in low esteem by the public at large. Meanwhile, in dictatorships they frequently churn out propaganda. In theory, western journalism prizes objectivity ("Comment is free, but facts are sacred," wrote C.P. Scott, editor of the *Guardian* newspaper, in 1921). In practice, this is not always the case: in the 1970s the American journalist Hunter S. Thompson (1937–2005) invented what became known as "Gonzo journalism", in which the journalist becomes a participant in the story and in which objectivity is no longer the essential aim. One feature of the internet age and the 21st century is the growth of "citizen journalism", in which members of the public, rather than trained journalists, disseminate the news and their views through new technologies, from internet blogs to cell-phone cameras.

Judaism The religion of the Jews, originating in a covenant around 2000BC between God and Abraham, the patriarch of the "children of Israel" and so founder of the Jewish nation. Judaism is the oldest of the Abrahamic religions (the others being Christianity and Islam), all of which believe in a single, omniscient and omnipotent god as creator and ruler of the universe. God's laws and commandments were revealed to Moses on Mount Sinai and recorded in the Torah. The various laws and regulations that define Jewish life and the relationship with God are contained in the Talmud, produced in two versions in the 3rd and 5th centuries AD. One feature of Judaism is its definition (as in "the Chosen People") of Jews by their ethnicity, regardless of whether they are believers or not (mainstream forms of Judaism do accept converts, but there is no **proselytism** and conversion is difficult). Another feature is the theme of exile; the earliest was to Egypt, from which Moses in 1313BC led them to the land of Israel (then known as Canaan). In 607BC the Babylonians dispersed the Jews from Israel and the same fate befell them in 70AD with the destruction of the Second Temple in Jerusalem by the Romans, resulting in a diaspora that eventually spread Jewish communities throughout the Arab world and Europe. There are various strains of Judaism today, ranging from ultra-Orthodox movements that reject the existence of modern Israel (on the grounds that the creation of a Jewish state must await the appearance of the messiah) to the liberal Reform Judaism common in the United States.

k

Kabbalism A Jewish tradition – the Kabbalah – of the mystical interpretation of the Bible, transmitted orally and claiming secret knowledge of the unwritten Torah that was given by God to Moses and Adam. This mystical approach to God led to accusations by some mainstream Jews that Kabbalism was pantheistic (see **pantheism**) and heretical. There were certainly elements of magic and cosmology, for example in the *Sefer Yetzira* (Book of Creation), appearing between the 3rd and 6th century and explaining creation as a process involving the ten divine numbers of God and the 22 letters of the Hebrew alphabet. The word itself comes from the Hebrew *qabbalah*, meaning tradition, and the origins of Kabbalism lie in 1st-century AD *merkavah* **mysticism**, following the 70AD destruction of the Second Temple in Jerusalem, where the aim was the ecstatic contemplation of the divine "chariot" (*merkavah*) seen in a vision by the prophet Ezekiel. The high point of the tradition came in the Middle Ages, as Kabbalism spread throughout the Jewish diaspora, especially among Jews expelled from Spain in 1492. In the 18th century it became influential among followers of the ultra-Orthodox Hasidic and Lubavitch sects. Practitioners of Kabbalah today include several celebrities, notably the singer Madonna.

Keynesianism A school of macroeconomics based on the work and ideas of the British economist John Maynard Keynes (1883–1946), especially *The General Theory of Employment, Interest and Money*, published in 1936. Keynesian economists argue that aggregate demand determines the level of real output; that the level of investment is not necessarily determined by the interest rate; that prices respond only slowly to changes in supply and demand, creating temporary gluts and shortages, especially of labour; and that economies can therefore settle with stubbornly high rates of unemployment. Central to the argument is the view that decisions by the private sector do not automatically lead to efficient macroeconomic outcomes – and from that it follows that governments, through fiscal policy, and central banks, through monetary policy, have roles to play in boosting demand in order to reduce unemployment. Reacting to the Great Depression of the 1930s, Keynes's solution was to stimulate the economy through lower interest rates and government investment in infrastructure – precisely the strategy later followed by most industrialised nations to counteract the "credit crunch" and global economic crisis that began in late 2008. Integral to this strategy is the Keynesian "multiplier effect": output will increase by a multiple of the original change in spending that caused it (that is, a \$10 billion increase in government spending might raise economic output by \$15 billion with a multiplier of 1.5). By contrast, the absence of government intervention can deepen a depression: if wages are cut in real terms to boost employment, demand will fall too, so reducing revenues and making investment in plant and equipment less likely.

Keynesian economists are not, however, uniform in their beliefs. While Keynes dismissed the "classical" notion that flexible prices automatically lead to increased demand and full employment, the so-called neo-Keynesians agree with more classical economists that the free market does have a tendency towards full employment (they blame persistently high unemployment on institutional rigidities and price rigidities). A second branch of Keynesians notes that in some instances an economy can be in such a state of "disequilibrium" that no amount of price flexibility will return it to full employment.

The main criticism of Keynesianism has come, especially in the inflationary decades of the 1970s and 1980s, from the monetarist followers of the American Nobel laureate Milton Friedman (1912–2006). They argue that rising inflation is the result of excessive money supply rather than increased aggregate demand, and that government intervention merely worsens the situation, with high inflation eroding savings and ensuring that boom is followed by bust (see **monetarism**). Another criticism came from Robert E. Lucas, Friedman's colleague at the University of Chicago, who noted that Keynesian policies were essentially short-term. To that Keynes had long ago had the answer: "In the long run, we are all dead."

Know-nothingism The anti-immigrant and anti-Roman
Catholic ideology and programme of the Know-nothing
Party (also called the American Party) that flourished in
the United States in the 1850s. Its origins lay in the
founding in 1849 in New York of the secret Order of the
Star-Spangled Banner in response to the rising
immigration of Germans in the mid-west and Irish in the
east, supposedly posing a threat to American-born
Protestants. The "Know-nothing" name came because
when its members were asked about the organisation,
they replied that they knew nothing. As membership
grew, so the name American Party was adopted, and by
1855 some 43 members of Congress belonged to it. That,
however, was the high point; soon afterwards anti-
slavery Know-nothings joined the Republican Party and
Know-nothings from the South joined the pro-slavery
Democratic Party.

L

Lacanianism The theories of Jacques Marie Emile Lacan (1901–81), a French psychoanalyst who reinterpreted the theories of Sigmund Freud (1856–1939), especially the theory of the subconscious, to take account of advances in linguistics and anthropology. Lacan argued that "the unconscious is structured like a language", and was therefore not a primitive part of the mind separated from the conscious. One Lacanian concept is that of "master signifiers" in language, words to which a subject's identity are most intimately bound. If someone identifies himself as a "communist", for example, an array of other signifiers – such as "freedom" or "democracy" – comes in a different sequence from that of someone identified as a "liberal".

Lamarckism A theory of evolution proposed by Jean-Baptiste Lamarck (1744–1829), a French naturalist, who held that traits acquired by an organism during its lifetime could be transmitted to its offspring. Lamarck, the first man to use the term "biology", wrote of a sequence of life forms rising like a series of staircases, with the organs of animals rising to higher levels as they became more complex. In his 1809 work *Philosophie Zoologique* he postulated two laws: that organs are improved with repeated use; and that such gains "are preserved by reproduction to the new individuals which arise". As an example, he cited how the forelegs and necks of giraffes became lengthened as they stretched to browse on trees. Some 50 years later, in his book *On the Origins of Species*, Charles Darwin called Lamarck's theory "pangenesis", and thought it might be a supplement to his own theory of natural selection. In the 1930s advances in genetics discredited Lamarckism in the view of most scientists.

Latitudinarianism The view that there should be no order of preference among varying forms of belief and worship. The word, from the Latin *latitudo* or "breadth", refers to the practices and tolerant attitude of a group of Anglican churchmen in the 17th and 18th centuries who opposed the dogmatic positions of the Church of England, arguing that reason, rather than tradition, should inform theology and be used to establish the certainty of Christian doctrines. As such, the Latitudinarians were the forerunners of the Broad Church movement in the 19th-century Church of England and of Congregationalists in America.

Leftism The ideology of left-wing politics, so-called because after the French Revolution of 1789 politicians supporting the republic and opposing the monarchy sat to the left of the president's chair. Leftists advocate social **egalitarianism** and, to varying degrees, government involvement in the economy. The leftist spectrum is broad, ranging from the "centre left" and social democracy to communism.

Legalism An adherence to law, especially its letter rather than its spirit.

Leninism Marxist ideology (see Marxism) as interpreted by the Russian revolutionary Vladimir Ilych Lenin (1870–1924), aiming at the dictatorship of the proletariat. To achieve this, capitalism must be overthrown by a disciplined party of professional revolutionaries, who would then educate the proletariat to abandon the ideas of religion and nationalism that had made the proletariat easy to exploit. Lenin also emphasised that, whatever the desirability of an international revolution, the victory of socialism could take place in one country at a time, declaring in 1918: "To wait until the toiling classes bring about a revolution on an international scale means that everybody should stand stock-still in expectation. That is nonsense." After Lenin's death, Joseph Stalin (1879–1953) and Leon Trotsky (1879–1940) fought for the leadership, not just of the new Union of Soviet Socialist Republics (USSR) but also of communism itself. Stalin, following the line laid down by Lenin, advocated "socialism in one country", meaning that the USSR should build socialism at home while supporting revolutionary governments abroad. Trotsky countered that socialism in one country was an impossibility, and that the USSR should be supporting permanent revolution everywhere, since genuine socialism in Russia would be possible only after the victory of the proletariat in the most important countries in Europe. Stalin won the argument, with Trotsky being driven into exile, and Marxism-Leninism – which Stalin's opponents simply called Stalinism – became the official ideology of the Soviet Union. The theory of Marxism-Leninism was that eventually the state would "wither away"; in practice this has never looked remotely possible in any communist country.

Lesbianism Female homosexuality: sexual or romantic desire between women. The term comes from the Greek island of Lesbos, home of Sappho, a 6th-century BC poetess, who declared her attraction to young women. There is no similar geographical epithet for male homosexuality.

Liberalism In politics, the state of being liberal, notably in emphasising the rights and freedom of the individual, usually with government guarantees for those rights and freedom. In North America and Britain, liberals are regarded as being to the left of centre, with their support, for example, of state welfare programmes. By contrast, the continental European definition puts liberals on the right, because of their support for the free market. In the American political debate to be a "liberal" may be to risk censure for being too close to socialism; yet in Australia the Liberal Party is essentially conservative. Liberalism can also be used in a religious context, indicating a freedom from traditional authority.

Libertarianism A political philosophy emphasising the liberty of the individual, with as little intervention as possible by the state in the affairs of the citizenry (which is why libertarians are at times associated with right-wing politics and at other times with anarchists – see anarchism). The guiding principle of libertarianism is "live and let live". The term was first used towards the end of the 18th century in debates pitting free will against determinism.

Libertinism The freedom from and therefore the disregard of conventional morality, especially sexual.

Literalism The adherence to the exact meaning of a word or phrase, without any allowance for metaphor or context – sometimes, therefore, leading to a certain confusion, though few would be misled if someone said: "There were millions of people waiting for the bus."

Localism A characteristic, such as an accent or idiom, peculiar to a particular locality. The word can also be used to refer to an excessive preference for a particular locality or region.

Logical positivism A school of philosophy, originating in the Vienna Circle of philosophers in the 1920s, that rejects the metaphysical and theological, holding instead that statements of fact are meaningful only if they can be verified and combining therefore empiricism with scientific rigour. Logical positivists were heavily influenced by the Austrian-British philosopher Ludwig Wittgenstein (1889–1951) and the British philosopher Bertrand Russell (1872–1970). Critics of logical positivism have pointed out that verifiability is impossible for negative or universal claims (for example, "not all ravens are black" and "all ravens are black"), and Karl Popper (1902–94), another Austrian-born British philosopher, argued that a better test would be falsifiability.

Lollardism The religious beliefs of the followers of John Wycliffe (c1330–84), a British theologian who criticised the Roman Catholic church and argued that the church should be poor, as in the earliest days of Christianity. The Lollards, who were soon condemned as heretics, were fundamentally anti-clerical, believing that the Roman Catholic church had been corrupted by power. By the 16th century and the English Reformation they had been absorbed into **Protestantism**.

Luddism (also Ludditism) A refusal to accept advances in technology, especially in the workplace. The term refers to the Luddites (perhaps named after Ned Ludd, a probably mythical participant in the destruction of machinery), bands of workers in the 19th century who, generally masked and acting at night, destroyed the new machines that threatened their jobs in Britain's cotton and woollen mills. The movement began near Nottingham, in the middle of England, in 1811 and soon spread to Yorkshire, Lancashire, Derbyshire and Leicestershire. In 1812 a band of Luddites was shot down under the orders of one employer, who was then murdered in retaliation. A mass trial of Luddites in 1813 resulted in hangings and deportations. There was renewed rioting in 1816 during the economic recession that followed the Napoleonic wars, but with a return to prosperity, and more repressive measures against belligerent workers, the movement faded. In the late 20th century the term was used in Britain to describe the opposition of print unions to the introduction of computerised typesetting in the newspaper industry.

Luminism A style of American painting in the latter half of the 19th century that emphasised the realistic depiction of light (*lumen* in Latin) and its effect on objects. The result, by artists such as FitzHugh Lane (1804–65), Martin Heade (1819–1904) and Frederic Edwin Church (1826–1900), was the painting of large seascapes and landscapes. The Luminists were influenced by what came to be known as the Hudson River School, so named for their paintings of the majestic scenery of New York's Hudson River and Catskill Mountains. The term Luminism was not coined until 1954, by John Baur, director of New York's Whitney Museum of American Art.

Lutheranism A Protestant denomination of Christianity that follows the doctrine of the German theologian Martin Luther (1483–1546), whose reforming zeal, exemplified in 1517 by *The Ninety-Five Theses on the Power and Efficacy of Indulgences*, divided Christianity in Europe and launched the Protestant Reformation. (Indulgences, remitting any punishment for sins already confessed, were sold by Roman Catholic clergy.) Luther argued that selling indulgences made a mockery of the notion of confession and penance. He taught that salvation comes by the grace of God alone, Christ having already paid for man's sins by his crucifixion, and he rejected Catholic insistence on priestly celibacy and the intermediary role of priests. Lutherans stress the primacy of the Bible as the church's authority; accept the sacraments of baptism and the Eucharist (but reject the idea of transubstantiation, in which the bread and wine of the Eucharist, commemorating Christ's last supper, become Christ's flesh and blood); and believe in predestination, with no freedom for the human will.

Lyricism The quality, from the Greek *lurikos*, meaning lyre, of being melodious, or the expression of blissful, sensual emotion.

Lysenkoism The ideas and policies of Trofim Denisovich Lysenko (1898–1976), a Ukrainian biologist and geneticist, who followed the theory of Jean-Baptiste Lamarck that evolution occurred by the inheritance of acquired characteristics (see Lamarckism). Lysenko, who opposed orthodox genetics but was director of the Institute of Genetics of the Academy of Sciences of the USSR from 1940 to 1965, was the dominant figure in Soviet agriculture, promising better and cheaper increases in crop yields than other biologists believed possible. At one point he claimed that wheat raised in an appropriate environment would produce rye seeds – the equivalent of saying that dogs in the wild could give birth to foxes. Lyskenko's fortunes varied with the political climate, and his ideas were discredited in favour of orthodox genetics after the fall from power of Nikita Khrushchev (1894–1971) in 1964.

m

Machiavellianism A doctrine of politics, or indeed of general
conduct, that considers morality irrelevant in the pursuit
or maintenance of power (and so considers any means,
however unscrupulous, permissible). The doctrine was
spelled out in *Il Principe* (The Prince), a treatise by Niccolò
Machiavelli (1469–1527), an Italian statesman, political
philosopher and civil servant of the Florentine republic.
As an example to instruct a new prince in how to wield
power, Machiavelli wrote: "If an injury has to be done to
a man, it should be so severe that his vengeance need not
be feared." Another example of Machiavelli's doctrine
has been taken to heart by many tyrannically inclined
rulers: "Since love and fear can hardly exist together, if
we must choose between them, it is far safer to be feared
than loved." "Machiavellianism" was first coined as a
pejorative term by the French in the 16th century, out of
their scorn for all things Italian. The same sense was
common in 16th-century England, for example in the
plays of Christopher Marlowe (c1564–93). *Il Principe* was
privately circulated by Machiavelli, and published only in
1532, five years after his death. In 1559 it and all

Machiavelli's works were placed on the Catholic church's *Index of Prohibited Books*, both because of Machiavelli's obvious scorn for the papacy and because of the books' celebration of amorality. As a term in psychology, Machiavellianism is a tendency to manipulate others for personal gain. Ironically, Machiavelli himself was apparently an upright citizen of Florence and a good and generous father to his family.

Malapropism The mistaken use of a word or phrase, with comic or ridiculous effect, as in George Bush (see **Bushism**): "We cannot let terrorists and rogue nations hold this nation hostile or hold our allies hostile." The word is derived from Mrs Malaprop, a character prone to such mistakes in *The Rivals*, a 1775 play by the Irish playwright Richard Brinsley Sheridan (1751–1816).

Malthusianism The theory that the population increases more rapidly than the supply of food, a process that then triggers famine, disease or war, leading in turn to a reduction in the population. The theory was spelled out in 1798 in *An Essay on the Principle of Population as it affects the Future Improvement of Society* by Thomas Robert Malthus (1766–1834), a British economist and demographer. Malthus, who was writing during the Industrial Revolution, was originally worried by the increase in poor and dependent people, arguing that charity to the poor would serve only to worsen the problem. Malthus's remedy for excessive population growth was premarital chastity, late marriage and sexual abstinence. History has proved the weakness of his exponential arithmetic, with agricultural and technological improvements able to feed a world population that Malthus could barely have imagined. Interestingly, an early critic of Malthus was Karl Marx, who dismissed Malthusianism as "schoolboyish" and "superficial".

Manichaeism A religious system (sometimes called Manichaeanism), combining Buddhism, Gnosticism, Zoroastrianism and other beliefs, founded in 3rd-century Persia by a prophet called Mani (c216–276), and positing a primeval conflict between light and dark, with matter – the material world – being regarded as dark and evil. Manichaeism thrived at least until the 7th century, spreading to China in the east and the Roman empire in the west, but had more or less died out by the 10th century. In a general sense the term is used today to mean a dualistic approach to belief (see dualism), the notion being that something is either black or white.

Mannerism A habitual gesture or way of speaking, in some cases so marked that it becomes an affectation. In the art world, it can refer to a style of painting and sculpture, characterised by complex perspective and lurid colours, developed in Italy in the 16th century and acting as a bridge between the Renaissance and the Baroque period. Benvenuto Cellini (1500–71) and El Greco (1541–1614) are both considered mannerists.

Maoism The communist ideology of Mao Zedong (1893–1976) in China. "Mao Zedong Thought", to use the official name, differed from conventional Marxism by replacing the urban proletariat (which China lacked) with an agrarian peasantry. Central to Maoism was the notion of permanent revolution and agricultural collectivisation. In practice, Maoism in China had tragic consequences, not least the famine-causing "Great Leap Forward" of the 1950s. Its anti-intellectualism also led to the disastrous decade, beginning in 1966, of the Cultural Revolution, during which the "Red Guards" of organised urban youth humiliated teachers and academics in their attack on "bourgeois things". In the decade of upheaval, millions of city-dwellers were sent to work in miserable circumstances in the rural hinterland, senior Communist Party figures such as Deng Xiaoping (1904–97) were purged and, in 1973, the "Gang of Four" (notably including Mao's third wife, Jiang Qing) gained political ascendancy. After Mao's death in 1976 the Gang of Four were accused of attempting to seize power and were imprisoned. Beyond China, Maoism has been adopted by several insurgent groups, for example in Peru and India. The Khmers Rouges implemented Maoism as the national ideology of Cambodia, with tragic, near-genocidal results during their period in power (1975–79).

Marxism The political and economic philosophy of the German philosopher Karl Marx (1818–83) and his compatriot Friedrich Engels (1820–95), arguing that class struggle will ultimately lead to a classless society and the overthrow of capitalism. Marxism is the underlying philosophy of communism, but Marx and Engels – who together published *The Communist Manifesto* in 1848

– themselves called their philosophy "scientific socialism". Marx saw the evolution of any society as the result of conflict between social classes: capitalism was a system in which the bourgeoisie, a minority of society, exploited the working proletariat, the vast majority. Marx postulated "three laws of capitalist development": the increasing accumulation of capital, the increasing concentration of capital, and the increasing misery of the proletariat – which would lead to a situation in which the proletariat would eventually rise in rebellion to seize the property of the capitalist class. The revolution would lead first to a transitional socialism and then to full communism. Marx explained the exploitation of the proletariat with his "labour theory of value": the value of a commodity should equal the labour time (which includes the inputs needed to feed, clothe and educate the worker) required to produce the commodity – so surplus value is the difference between the value produced and the value received by the worker, with the capitalist taking surplus value from the worker. The capitalist could then invest this surplus in labour-saving machinery, so driving down wages and worsening the plight of the proletariat. Marx died before any of his ideas could be tested, which is perhaps why Marxism in practice has emerged in several different varieties, for example Marxism-Leninism, Trotskyism and Maoism.

Marxism-Leninism See Leninism.

Masochism The derivation of pleasure, especially sexual, from one's own pain or humiliation. The term is derived from the name of Leopold von Sacher-Masoch (1835–1895), an Austrian author, who wrote of his pleasure from being beaten and belittled. It was first used in 1886 by the Austrian psychiatrist Richard von Krafft-Ebing (1840–1902), who wrote: "I feel justified in calling this sexual anomaly 'Masochism', because the author Sacher-Masoch frequently made this perversion, which up to his time was quite unknown to the scientific world as such, the substratum of his writings." Masochism and sadism (sexual pleasure through inflicting pain on others) frequently go together, but the term "masochism" can also be used in a metaphorical (and less painful) sense, as in "working so much overtime is a form of masochism".

Materialism An emphasis on material possessions, implying that they are more important than intangible, spiritual values. In philosophy, materialism is the notion that nothing exists other than matter, and that everything – including the activities of the mind – is therefore the result of material agencies. In Marxist theory, borrowed from the German philosopher Georg Hegel (1770–1831), dialectical materialism is the idea that change results from the conflict of opposites: thesis and antithesis lead to synthesis.

Mazdaism Another term for Zoroastrianism, from Ahura Mazda, the supreme deity of the Persian religion.

McCarthyism The practice of making politically charged accusations of disloyalty or treason, often on the basis of little or, indeed, no evidence. The term, coined in 1950,

comes from the zeal of Senator Joseph McCarthy
(1908–57) in pursuing alleged communists and "fellow
travellers" in America (including in its government
bodies) in the wake of the second world war, notably
through his role in the Senate Permanent Subcommittee
on Investigations. Some of the most famous instances of
McCarthyism were the interrogations of Hollywood
actors and film-makers before the House Committee on
Un-American Activities, resulting in an unofficial blacklist
of hundreds, including figures such as the screenwriter
Ring Lardner junior, the actor and director Orson Welles,
and the actor and singer Paul Robeson. Eventually
opinions turned against McCarthy, with the CBS
newscaster Edward R. Murrow saying on air: "We must
not confuse dissent with disloyalty. We must remember
always that accusation is not proof and that conviction
depends upon evidence and due process of law." The
final blow for McCarthy came in the Senate
Subcommittee on Investigations in televised hearings in
1954 pitting the US army against McCarthy, when the
attorney for the army said to McCarthy: "Have you no
sense of decency, sir? At long last, have you left no sense
of decency?"

Mechanism An assembly of moving parts enabling a machine
to function, or the process by which something happens.
As a philosophical term, mechanism is the idea that all
phenomena have a mechanical explanation.

Meliorism The idea that the world can be made better
through human effort. The term, from the Latin *melior*,

meaning better, was possibly coined by the British writer George Eliot (1819–80) in her letters published in 1877. In politics, meliorism described a faction of the Italian Communist Party led by Giorgio Napolitano. Its goal was to improve Italy's capitalist society through gradual reform rather than revolution. The left wing of the Communist Party used the term derisively. After the dissolution of the Italian Communist Party in 1991, most meliorists, including Napolitano, became members of the Democratic Party of the Left.

Menshevism The ideology of the Mensheviks (from Russian, meaning "people of the minority"), members of the non-Leninist wing of the Russian Social Democratic Workers' Party. The Leninist wing was composed of the Bolsheviks ("people of the majority" – see Bolshevism), with the split occurring at a party congress in 1903 when one group opposed Lenin's plan for a small, disciplined party of professional revolutionaries, preferring instead a mass party on the lines of west European social democratic parties. Lenin's supporters gained a temporary majority (hence "Bolshevik") on the central committee; their opponents, led by L. Martov (the pseudonym of Yuli Osipovich Zederbaum, 1873–1923), were promptly termed Mensheviks. Unlike the Bolsheviks, the Mensheviks considered that backward Russia could not pass directly to a dictatorship of the proletariat but should pass through a transitional phase of bourgeois control. In 1912 the Mensheviks and Bolsheviks formally became separate parties. During the first world war the Bolsheviks hoped for the defeat of tsarist Russia and the development of an international civil war. By contrast, the Mensheviks were divided: rightist Mensheviks supported Russia's war effort; the left called for pacifism. Following the 1917 Russian revolution, the Mensheviks tried to form a legal opposition, but by 1921 they were suppressed by the new Russian Communist Party, heirs of the Bolsheviks.

Mercantilism The belief that a nation's wealth is enhanced by exporting as much as possible while importing as little as possible. As such, mercantilism often leads to government intervention and protectionism. As an economic theory the mercantile system, which identified national wealth with the accumulation of precious metals, was dominant during the imperialist expansion of European powers from the 16th to the 18th century (see imperialism). Acceptance of mercantilism began to fade at the end of the 18th century, under the influence of the free-market ideas of Adam Smith (1723–90), but it remains popular with non-economists – especially vote-seeking politicians reluctant to challenge an electorate's protectionist instinct.

Mesmerism Generally, a state of fascination; but specifically, the system of hypnosis, through "animal magnetism", developed by Franz Anton Mesmer (1734–1815), a German physician. Mesmer claimed to be able to treat a variety of ailments by "channelling" a magnetic force supposedly residing in the bodies of animate beings. In 1784 a panel of scientists commissioned by the French king, Louis XVI, concluded that any benefit from Mesmer's treatments was due to "imagination". Nonetheless, his notion of unseen internal forces continues to have some support (not least with the influence of traditional Chinese medicine) and Mesmer is often credited with laying the foundations of modern hypnotherapy.

Metabolism The physical and chemical processes within an organism that enable it to maintain life. Constructive metabolism stores energy by synthesising proteins, carbohydrates and fats; destructive metabolism, breaking substances down, produces energy and waste.

Methodism The doctrine of the Methodist movement of Protestant Christianity, originating in the *General Rules* issued in 1743 by John Wesley (1703-91) and his brother Charles (1707-88), British Anglican theologians critical of the Church of England's lack of energy. The Methodists, who now number around 70m in various denominations around the world, broke away from the Anglican church after the death of John Wesley in 1791. Methodism, which has a strong evangelical tradition (see **evangelicalism**), stresses personal morality and follows the view of Jacobus Arminius (1560-1609), a Dutch Protestant who argued that Christ died for all men rather than just for the elect (see **Arminianism**). In particular, Methodism differs from **Calvinism** in rejecting the notion of predestination (John Wesley said such an idea viewed "God as worse than the devil").

Militarism The belief that a nation is best served by having a strong military. The word tends to be used pejoratively, often being associated with imperialism and bellicosity, be it the Roman empire, Germany in the first world war or Japan in the first half of the 20th century.

Millenarianism Another word for millennialism.

Millennialism Also known as millenarianism, the word refers in general to a period of 1,000 years, but more particularly to the belief in 1,000 years of bliss during which Christ, after the "second coming" predicted in the Bible's Book of Daniel and the Book of Revelation, will rule on earth. This idea is central to several Christian and quasi-Christian religious groups, including Jehovah's Witnesses, Plymouth Brethren, Adventists and Mormons. The fascination with a 1,000-year period predates Christianity, being found in early Jewish thought, and the notion was also a feature of medieval Zoroastrianism.

Minimalism The process or effect of reducing something to its essential form. In the arts, minimalism was a movement of sculpture and painting, beginning in the 1950s in New York and popular in the 1960s and 1970s, that emphasised the simplification of form, using primary colours and excluding personal expression by the artist. This school was also known as "ABC art", and its practitioners included Ellsworth Kelly and Agnes Martin (1912–2004). Minimalism in music is characterised by a repetitious, simplified pattern of trance-inducing rhythms, often influenced by music from Asia. Probably the best-known exponents are the Americans Philip Glass – though he does not accept the term for his later music

– and John Cage (1912–92). In literature, the Japanese *haiku* – three lines of five, seven and five syllables – is a good example of minimalism, but there is surely nothing to beat Samuel Beckett's 30-second play *Breath*, first performed in 1969, containing neither characters nor words (though the stage was to be littered with "miscellaneous rubbish").

Mithraism The worship of Mithra (known to the Romans as Mithras), the greatest of gods in Persia before the 6th-century BC arrival of Zoroastrianism. Mithra was the god of the sun but also the god of mutual obligation between a king and his soldiers – and so was the god of war and justice. The most important ritual of Mithraism was the sacrifice of a bull, whose blood then was supposed to fertilise the earth. Mithra was first mentioned in Indian mythology around 1400BC, and the worship of Mithra then went north to Persia and subsequently spread through the Hellenic world. In the 2nd and 3rd centuries AD the cult of Mithra was popular among Roman soldiers and was a rival to Christianity (indeed, some of its ritual – for example, the idea of wine turning into blood at the sacrifice of the bull – has an obvious resemblance to Christian tradition). The Roman emperor Commodus (ruling from 180 to 192) was a believer in Mithraism but the religion rapidly declined when Constantine I accepted Christianity in 337 (although a later emperor, Julian, ruling from 361 to 363, abandoned Christianity and may well have been an initiate to Mithraism – hence the common description of him as "Julian the Apostate").

Modernism A liking for what is modern, especially in the arts, and therefore a break with tradition. In painting, modernism began in the late 19th century and so embraces artists as different as the French Edouard Manet (1832–83) and the American Jackson Pollock (1912–56). In the late 20th century modernism was followed by postmodernism – a hard-to-define concept that could mean reintroducing classical elements or taking modern styles to an extreme. Modernism can also refer to movements to adapt the beliefs and behaviour of the Christian church, be it through liberal theology in 20th-century Protestantism or new interpretations of faith and doctrine among Roman Catholics in the 19th and 20th centuries. Modernists were sceptical of miracles and, while arguing that the Bible was the only authoritative source, nonetheless advocated a "rationalist" approach to Biblical stories and an acceptance that doctrines could evolve. Pope Pius X was not impressed, in 1907 condemning modernism as the "synthesis of all heresies".

Monarchism Belief in having a monarch (derived from the Greek for a single ruler), be it king or queen, emperor or empress, as ruler of a country. A monarch may be an absolute ruler – the norm in Europe in the Middle Ages – or a constitutional monarch, with virtually no powers other than ceremonial. The hereditary principle, with succession to the throne taking place within a royal family, is usually thought of as intrinsic to a monarchy, though the positions of Roman emperors, Holy Roman emperors and kings of Poland were at least nominally non-hereditary. The French revolutions of the 18th and 19th centuries and the two world wars of the 20th century meant a decline of monarchism and a rise in republicanism in Europe, but those monarchies that have survived – for example, in Belgium, the Netherlands and Sweden – have become symbols of national identity. The British monarch (whose absolute power was surrendered in the 17th century) is also monarch of several parts of what was the British empire, such as Canada and Australia. Absolute monarchy, since the overthrow of the king of Nepal in 2008, is now confined mainly to Saudi Arabia, the Arab states of the Gulf and Brunei.

Monasticism The religious practice of renouncing the world and its comforts in order to live a life of spiritual contemplation and celibacy in a monastery (a community of fellow believers, or monks; the female equivalent is of nuns living together in a convent). St Anthony of Egypt (c251–356) founded early Christian monasteries in the Egyptian desert, and monasticism spread quickly throughout the Byzantine empire from the 4th century onwards. But monasticism (from the Greek *monastikos*, in turn from *monazein*, meaning to live alone) predates Christianity by several centuries, with individual hermits being found in India as long ago as 1500BC and groups of hermits existing in Hinduism and Jainism from around 600BC. Meanwhile, Buddhism has had a monastic tradition for the past two-and-a-half millennia, though avoiding the extremes of self-mortification that some Christian monastic orders practice.

Monetarism A theory of economics, developed mainly by
Milton Friedman (1912–2006) and colleagues at the
University of Chicago, that holds that controlling the
supply of money is the best method of stabilising an
economy. The theory, which drew mainstream attention
following work by Friedman in the 1950s and 1960s,
argues that a moderate growth in the money supply leads
to a moderate growth in the economy with only low
inflation. The basic arithmetic is that the supply of
money multiplied by the velocity of its turnover (how
many times it is spent) equals the price of goods or
services multiplied by their quantity. If the money supply
is increased but the velocity remains the same, either the
price of goods will increase or their quantity will. By this
logic, if the money supply is increased, people will have
money surplus to their needs and will spend it. Equally, if
the money supply is reduced, people will lessen their
spending in order to maintain or rebuild their reserves of
money. Monetarism was in many ways a reaction to
Keynesianism (Keynes had famously declared that
"money does not matter") and became politically
influential with the apparent failure of Keynesianism to
explain the simultaneous rise in the 1970s of
unemployment and inflation. The result was the
monetarist stringency in the United States of successive
Federal Reserve chairmen, Paul Volcker and Alan
Greenspan, and the "supply-side" economic philosophies
of the American president, Ronald Reagan (1911–2004),
and the British prime minister, Margaret Thatcher. Critics
of monetarism argue that the cost in unemployment, as a
result of inflation-busting high interest rates, was

excessive. Following the credit-crunch-induced global economic crisis that began in late 2008, the Keynesian policy of financial stimulus by governments (automatically increasing the money supply) regained its popularity, but the monetarist-inspired practice of targeting a low inflation rate remains a staple of most central banks.

Monism The doctrine in philosophy or theology that denies dualism or pluralism. There is, therefore, no distinction between mind and matter, and there is only one supreme being – however much, in Hinduism for example, appearances may be to the contrary.

Monophysitism The doctrine that Jesus Christ was of one, divine nature, rather than the two natures – divine and human – held by the doctrine of Nestorianism and asserted by Christianity's Council of Chalcedon (the church's fourth ecumenical meeting) in Turkey in 451. The notion of monophysitism (from the Greek *monos*, meaning single, and *phusis*, meaning nature) was central to the teaching of Eutyches (c380–455), a monk in Constantinople who argued that Christ's divine nature absorbed his humanity. An attempt to reconcile monophysitism with Christian orthodoxy was proposed in 622 with the doctrine of monotheletism, which argued that Christ had two natures but operated with one will. However, this was condemned as a heresy at the Third Council of Constantinople in 680, so preserving the schism between monophysitism and orthodoxy. Denominations that remain followers of the monophysite doctrine are the Coptic church in Egypt, the Jacobite church of Syria and the Armenian church.

Monopolism The practice of gaining or having exclusive control of a product, service or market. A monopoly (from the Greek *monos*, meaning single, and *polein*, meaning sell) can be the result of one business driving out competitors or, in the words of the economist Milton Friedman, it may arise "from government support or from collusive agreements among individuals". Either way, the lack of competition will probably lead to higher prices and lower quality. As a result, developed economies invariably have anti-monopoly legislation (for example, the antitrust laws in America), their aim being not just to prevent a monopoly but more usually to combat cartels. In practice, most countries define as a monopolist any firm having a dominant position, for example more than one-third of a market. This has led to adverse court judgments, in both the United States and the European Union, for the American company Microsoft on the grounds that it had abused its dominant position in some areas of computer software. One area in which monopolism is common is that of public utilities, with water, for example, often being considered a "natural monopoly". In such cases, the safeguard against abuse is government regulation. In the 1980s Margaret Thatcher's government in Britain deregulated and "privatised" several so-called natural monopolies, a process that was imitated elsewhere as other governments sought to raise money by selling state-owned utilities.

Monotheism The belief that there is only one God or
supreme being. Examples are the Abrahamic religions:
Judaism, Christianity and Islam, though Baha'ism, too, is
sometimes described as an Abrahamic religion. The
contrast is with **polytheism** (the belief in many gods), but
some might argue that the Christian concept of the
Trinity (God is simultaneously Father, Son and Holy
Spirit) somewhat strains the concept of monotheism.
Judaism and Islam entertain no such notions of plurality.

Monotheletism (or monothelitism) A theological doctrine,
first proposed in 622 and immediately embraced by the
Byzantine emperor Heraclius (c575–641, emperor from
610), that argued that Jesus Christ, though having two
natures (divine and human), had only one will.
Monotheletism (from the Greek *monos*, meaning single
and *theletes*, meaning "one that wills") was an attempt to
reconcile the monophysite heresy, which taught that
Christ had only one – divine – nature, with the
established doctrine that he had two natures, divine and
human, in one person (see **monophysitism**). In 638
Heraclius proclaimed monotheletism as the empire's
official form of Christianity, but this led to such
controversy that his successor, Constans II (630–68,
emperor from 641), issued an edict in 648 forbidding any
discussion of the question. Constantine IV (c652–85,
emperor from 668), however, did not sympathise with
monotheletism and in 680 summoned the Third Council
of Constantinople, which condemned the doctrine as a
heresy and upheld the orthodox Catholic view that
Christ had two wills, divine and human, corresponding

to his two natures. This led to the disappearance of monotheletism, except in the Maronite church of Syria and Lebanon.

Montanism A heretical Christian movement, both millenarian and ascetic, founded by Montanus, a self-styled prophet, in Phrygia, Turkey, in the middle of the 2nd century (see **millenarianism** and **asceticism**). Montanus, a recent convert to Christianity, appeared in Ardabau, a small Phrygian village, in about 156, falling into a trance and prophesying under the apparent influence of the Holy Spirit. Montanus was joined by two young women, Prisca and Maximillia, who also made prophetic utterances in a trance with the collective message that Judgment Day was imminent. Montanism spread rapidly through Asia Minor and at first did not seem to threaten Catholic authority – not least because prophecy was held in high esteem in the early church. However, theological conflict was inevitable: whereas Catholics held that a sinner's repentance restored him or her to grace, the Montanists believed that a Christian fallen from grace could never be redeemed. Montanus also claimed to have a final revelation of the Holy Spirit, implying that the church would have to accept additions to the teachings of Christ and the Apostles. In about 177 the Catholic bishops of Asia Minor, fearing the rise of a Montanist hierarchy, excommunicated the Montanists. Nonetheless, Montanism continued in Asia Minor until it was crushed by Emperor Justinian I, who ruled from 527 to 565 and sent John of Ephesus to destroy the Montanist shrine at Pepuza, a Phrygian village where Montanus had predicted the Messiah would appear. Asia Minor, however, was not the only region where Montanism has thrived. The doctrine was also important in Carthage, in what is now Tunisia, where the theologian Tertullian (c160–225) became interested in Montanism around 206, finally leaving the Catholic church in 212 and railing against its "laxity".

Moral absolutism The ethical doctrine that some actions are absolutely right or wrong, regardless of their context or consequences. The doctrine is in contrast to consequentialism (where the value of an action is judged by its consequences). It differs, too, from moral universalism, which argues that the same things are right and wrong for all people, but not necessarily in all contexts. Moral absolutism is fundamental to many religions, in particular the Abrahamic religions of Judaism, Christianity and Islam, and underlies the philosophy of the German philosopher Immanuel Kant (1724–1804), who once declared: "Do what is right, though the world may perish."

Moralism The practice of making moral judgments, especially about someone else's behaviour. The basis of such judgments is the idea of morality, the code that determines right from wrong.

Moral objectivism See moral universalism.

Moral relativism The view in ethics that what is right or wrong is not absolute but depends on the circumstances and context. The notion has existed throughout history, and in different cultures. Human sacrifice, for example, was acceptable to the Aztecs but considered murder in most societies. The Greek historian Herodotus observed in the 5th century BC that each society has its own values and way of behaving. The Dutch philosopher Baruch Spinoza (1632–77) argued that nothing is inherently good or evil. Moral relativism offends fundamentalist Jews, Christians and Muslims, who all see God's laws as absolute (see fundamentalism). Other critics, for example of the oppression of women by the Afghan Taliban, argue that it provides an excuse for behaviour that should be universally unacceptable.

Moral universalism An ethical doctrine, also known as moral objectivism, that is similar to moral absolutism in holding that actions are right or wrong for all people – but not, in contrast to moral absolutism, necessarily regardless of their context.

Mormonism A religion, properly known as the Church of Jesus Christ of Latter-day Saints, founded in America in 1830 by Joseph Smith (1805–44), who claimed to have received a vision in 1823 of a heavenly messenger, Moroni, revealing the existence of a buried book of golden plates written by ancient American prophets. Once translated into English, these plates became the Book of Mormon, an account of God's relationship with the two great races of prehistoric Americans – the Jaredites, who were led from the Tower of Babel in Babylon, and the Nephites, who came from Jerusalem.

According to the Book of Mormon, America is the "Land of Zion", awaiting the second coming of the Messiah. The Book of Mormon and the Bible are two of the four books fundamental to Mormonism, which mixes mainstream Christianity with the revelations and teachings of Smith and other Mormon leaders. After Smith's death in 1844, most members of his church chose Brigham Young (1801–77) as their leader and joined him on a migration eastwards to what is now Utah, the centre of modern Mormonism. A controversial feature of 19th-century Mormonism was the practice of polygamy. This was officially abandoned in 1890, but groups of Mormon fundamentalists continue to practise the custom, in defiance of both the law and the official church. The church has records of more than 13.5m members, but churchgoers are thought to number under 5m.

Muggletonianism A religious movement of the followers of Lodowicke Muggleton (1608–98), a British Puritan, and his cousin, John Reeve (1608–58). After claiming to have spiritual revelations in 1651, the two men, both London tailors, declared themselves to be the two witnesses referred to in the Old Testament's Book of Revelation (Rev. 11:3–6). They preached that the distinction between the three persons of the triune God (the Father, the Son and the Holy Spirit) was purely nominal; that God had a human body; and that, leaving Moses and the prophet Elijah in charge in heaven, he himself descended to die on the Cross. The unforgivable sin, according to Muggleton and Reeve, was to reject them as true prophets. Not surprisingly, Muggletonianism, though

neither evangelical nor political, attracted opposition.
Muggleton himself was imprisoned for blasphemy in
1653 and in 1677 he was fined £500 for blasphemy.
Despite its eccentric nature, Muggletonianism survived
into the late 19th century, and may well, according to
some scholars, have influenced the visionary British artist
and poet William Blake (1757–1827).

Multiculturalism A belief in the benefits of cultural diversity
within a society. This has long been a matter of historical
fact in ethnically diverse countries such as India,
Indonesia, Malaysia and Singapore. More recently it has
been invoked by several western countries – for example,
Canada and Britain – as a way of accepting immigrants
and their descendants into the host society. Its success,
however, is a matter of debate, with critics – for example,
in the Netherlands – saying multiculturalism sustains and
worsens racial tensions and divisions in society. France,
by contrast, has always steadfastly pursued a policy of
monoculturalism: because all French people are equal,
the government refuses even to count ethnic minorities
or to embrace American-style policies of affirmative
action and positive discrimination.

Multilateralism A relationship, especially in international
politics, that involves three or more countries
(**bilateralism** would involve just two, and **unilateralism**
only one). The term therefore relates to international
institutions such as the United Nations and its various
bodies. Although most multilateral institutions date from
after the second world war, there are earlier examples: at

the Congress of Vienna, for example, in 1814–15, European powers redrew the national boundaries of Europe after the Napoleonic wars; similarly, in 1919 the victorious nations at the end of the first world war worked together to impose the Treaty of Versailles on Germany, and then to found the League of Nations (an unsuccessful forerunner of the UN). Recent examples of multilateralism include the Kyoto Protocol on climate change, drawn up in 1997, and the International Criminal Court, founded in 2002. Neither found favour with the administration of President George W. Bush, leading to accusations of American unilateralism.

Mutualism The idea that a shared dependency helps social well-being. In economics, mutualism is associated with the ideas of the French anarchist philosopher Pierre-Joseph Proudhon (1809–65). Mutualism is an aspect of the labour theory of value, popularised by Adam Smith (1723–90): when labour or its product is sold, it ought to receive in exchange goods or services equivalent to "the amount of labour necessary to produce an article of exactly similar and equal utility", as Francis Tandy put it in his 1896 book, *Voluntary Socialism.* Anything less would amount to exploitation or usury. An example of the theory in business is the mutual company, where no shares are issued and the company is owned by those members doing business with it (as remains the case with a few building societies in Britain). In biology, mutualism is a type of symbiosis, being an association between the organisms of two different species from which each benefits. An example is the presence of rumen bacteria in cattle: the bacteria live in the cow's digestive tract and help the cow digest the plants it has eaten.

Mysticism The pursuit of spiritual truths, especially those attained through meditation, that are beyond the normal reach of the intellect. Mysticism, though rarely part of mainstream religious practice, is found in many religions: Islam, for example, has its Sufi mystics, and Judaism its Kabbalism.

n

Narcissism An excessive interest in oneself and one's appearance – in common parlance, extreme vanity. The word was first used in the late 19th century; Havelock Ellis (1859–1939), a British sexologist of the era, for example, described excessive masturbation as "Narcissus-like". It is derived from the classical Greek fable of Narcissus, a handsome youth who rejected the advances of the nymph Echo and as a punishment was made to fall in love with his own reflection. Unable to consummate his love, Narcissus faded away, turning into the flower that bears his name. In the 1960s psychologists and psychiatrists began to diagnose "narcissistic personality disorder", although Sigmund Freud (1856–1939) had in 1914 argued that a degree of narcissism was part of a healthy personality. Baby-boomers will doubtless connect narcissism with the lyrics of a 1972 pop song by Carly Simon: "You're so vain, I'll bet you think this song is about you."

Nationalism A political ideology, in some ways close to patriotism or even jingoism and chauvinism, that emphasises the nation. The term was used as early as the late 18th century by the German philosopher Johann Gottfried von Herder (1744-1803), but nationalism's rise to prominence was prompted mostly by the French Revolution. In the 20th century nationalism was invariably the force successfully impelling subject peoples to seek their independence from Europe's colonial powers – for example, the struggles of Vietnam and Algeria against French rule, or Kenya's insurrection against the British. Modern examples of nationalism include the Palestinians' goal of an independent state and the desire of the ETA movement to establish a Basque state separate from Spain. In recent years in Europe, nationalism has often been identified in a pejorative sense with the extreme right (for example, the British National Party or France's Front National), whose concept of the nation usually excludes immigrants and ethnic minorities.

National Socialism The political doctrine of the Nazi Party in Germany (see Nazism).

Naturalism A style of representation that emphasises accuracy and realism. The term was applied to a 19th-century artistic and literary movement that included the French painter Théodore Rousseau (1812-67) and his compatriot, the novelist Emile Zola (1840-1902). In philosophy, naturalism is a school of thought that rejects the supernatural.

Naturism A movement defined by its adherents as a lifestyle
in harmony with nature and expressed by nudity. The
concept was first defined in 1778 by Jean Baptiste Luc
Planchon (1734–81), a Belgian doctor who advocated
naturism as a way of improving health. Naturism,
presumably for fear of embarrassment, has never been a
mass movement, but it gained a degree of popularity in
Germany in the early 20th century. Today, naturist
holiday camps and beaches are found in many countries.
For most people, naturism and nudism are
interchangeable words, but some will argue that whereas
naturism is a lifestyle without clothes, nudism is simply
the act of being naked.

Nazism The ideology, known in German properly as National
Socialism (*Nationalsozialismus*), of Adolf Hitler's fascist
National Socialist German Workers' Party (the Nazi Party),
which was formed at the end of the first world war,
originally as the German Workers' Party (DAP), by the
nationalist Anton Drexler (1884–1942) in reaction to the
reparations imposed on Germany by the Versailles treaty
of 1919. Hitler (1889–1945) was the DAP's 55th member.
Nazism was characterised by authoritarian nationalism
and a racist ideology that preached the superiority of
"Aryan" Germans – hence the extreme anti-Semitism that
led to the Holocaust. In free elections in 1932 the Nazi
Party emerged with the most votes, leading to Hitler's
appointment as chancellor in January 1933, followed by
12 years of dictatorship (all other political parties having
been banned in 1933) until Germany's defeat in the
second world war.

In economic policy, the Nazi Party employed central planning for both the agricultural and industrial sectors, rapidly increasing the country's economic output (much of it under the control – actual or threatened – of the state). In 1927 Hitler had said: "We are socialists. We are enemies of today's capitalistic economic system for the exploitation of the economically weak, with its unfair salaries, with its unseemly evaluation of a human being according to wealth and property, instead of responsibility and performance." Two years later, however, Hitler confessed that socialism was "an unfortunate word altogether" to have used, and in 1931 he said: "I want everyone to keep what he has earned, subject to the principle that the good of the community takes priority over that of the individual. But the state should retain control; every owner should feel himself to be an agent of the state." What remained constant was Hitler's demagogic populism. Foreign policy, meanwhile, was dominated by the ideal of pan-Germanism and so a "Greater Germany" (*Grossdeutschland*), which inevitably meant a push for military conquest to gain "living room" (*Lebensraum*) for the ethnically German peoples. After Germany's defeat the Nazi Party was banned, but its racist and anti-Semitic doctrine lives on in the extreme right-wing politics of "neo-Nazis" in America (the American Nazi Party has existed since 1959) and several European countries. Rather bizarrely, Israel in 2008 experienced anti-Semitic violence and vandalism by a group of young Russian immigrants espousing Nazism.

Neocatastrophism See catastrophism.

Neoclassicism A school of art, literature, theatre, music or architecture that emulates the cultural products of ancient Greece and ancient Rome. Neoclassicism began in Rome in the mid-18th century as a reaction to the baroque and rococo styles. A prime exponent of neoclassical painting was Jacques-Louis David (1748–1825), with his works glorifying the French Revolution and Napoleon Bonaparte. In music the term also refers to the return in the 20th century by composers such as Igor Stravinsky (1882–1971) and Benjamin Britten (1913–76) to the styles of the 17th and 18th centuries, this time as a reaction to 19th-century romanticism. Although neoclassicism's dominance in architecture had faded by the mid-19th century, its influence has lived on, for example in the buildings of "traditional" architects such as the British Quinlan Terry.

Neoconservatism A political and social philosophy (literally "new" or "newly" conservative) that advocates free-market economics and the robust use of power, including military might, to spread democracy and promote human rights. "Neo-cons", as its adherents are known, exist in several countries but their origins are essentially American. One source was a group of intellectuals, notably Irving Kristol (1920–2009) and Nathan Glazer, who studied at the City College of New York in the late 1930s. Kristol famously described a neo-con as "a liberal mugged by reality" (many neo-cons had once been liberals, and Kristol had even been a Trotskyite). Another source was Leo Strauss (1899–1973), a German-American political scientist at the University of Chicago. In contrast to traditional paleoconservatives (see **paleoconservatism**), neo-cons are in favour of globalisation and take a liberal stance on issues such as immigration, abortion, homosexuality and religious differences.

Neoconservatism first became politically influential in the 1980s with the Reagan presidency (and also, in Britain, with the Thatcher years), and was arguably the dominant strand of thought during the presidency of George W. Bush, with neo-cons such as Paul Wolfowitz and Richard Perle pressing strongly for the invasion of Iraq in 2003. The power of the neo-cons has been diminished by the depressing reality of the Iraq war and its aftermath, and by the return to government in the United States of the Democrats. Nonetheless, neo-cons such as William Kristol (son of Irving) remain influential in Republican circles.

Neo-Darwinism A theory of evolution that combines Darwin's ideas of natural selection with the findings of genetics first espoused by the Austrian scientist Gregor Mendel (1822–84) in the 19th century. Ironically, the term was first used by George Romanes (1848–94), a Canadian-born British biologist, to refer to the idea that evolution occurs through natural selection alone. In its modern sense, as the so-called "modern evolutionary synthesis", neo-Darwinism dates from the mid-20th century, with most scientists accepting that Mendelian genetics is compatible with natural selection and gradual evolution.

Neo-interventionism The doctrine by which one state or collection of states are justified in taking military action in another state on the basis that human rights transcend sovereignty. It was used in support of the NATO bombing campaign in 1999 to force Serbia to abandon its attempt to wrest the former Yugoslavian province of Kosovo from the control of ethnic Albanian Kosovars. The NATO campaign was carried out without the permission of the UN. Another example was Britain's military intervention in 2000 in Sierra Leone to evacuate foreign nationals and hasten an end to the country's civil war.

Neoliberalism A political and economic ideology that seeks to marry an emphasis on free markets and economic growth with traditional liberal concerns for social justice. The term was coined in 1938 by Alexander Rüstow (1885–1963), a German sociologist and economist, who was one of the theorists of the "social market economy" that helped Germany recover from the second world war. However, the modern sense of neoliberalism, in which concern for social justice is less prominent, dates from the 1980s and the economic policies of Margaret Thatcher in Britain and Ronald Reagan (1911–2004) in America, both of them influenced by the free-market ideas that had come after the second world war from the Austrian-born British economist Friedrich Hayek (1899–1992) and from economists such as Milton Friedman (1912–2006) at the university of Chicago (where Hayek, normally associated with the London School of Economics, also taught). In seeking to minimise the role of the state, neoliberalism stands in contrast to Keynesianism and became popular in large part because of the failure of Keynesian policies to solve the various economic crises of the 1970s. Neoliberalism is often linked to the "Washington

Consensus" (a term coined in 1989 by a British economist, John Williamson, to describe the reforms – such as austerity programmes, trade liberalisation, deregulation and privatisation – that were the standard remedy advanced to developing countries in economic crisis by the Washington DC-based IMF, World Bank and US Treasury Department).

Neologism A newly coined word (from the Greek *neos*, meaning new, and *logos*, meaning word) that may, or may not, enter into common usage. Presumably neologism was itself once a neologism, and indeed the *Oxford English Dictionary* dates the use of the word in print back to 1772. A 20th-century neologism was internet; podcast is an example from the 21st century. The rarest neologism would, by definition, be a *hapax legomenon* (a direct transliteration of the Greek for "once said"): a word used only once.

Neoplasticism A movement in Dutch art founded in 1917 by Theo van Doesburg (1883–1931), who propagated the movement's ideas in a journal called *De Stijl* (The Style), which was the original name of the movement. The style in question was a pure abstraction, using only vertical and horizontal lines in black, white, grey and primary colours. *De Stijl* came to be known as neoplasticism – the new plastic art or *Nieuwe Beelding* in Dutch – and its most famous exponent was Piet Mondrian (1872–1944), who in a letter in 1914 had written: "I construct lines and colour combinations on a flat surface, in order to express general beauty with the utmost awareness. Nature (or, that which I see) inspires me, puts me, as with any painter, in an emotional state so that an urge comes about to make something, but I want to come as close as possible to the truth and abstract everything from that, until I reach the foundation (still just an external foundation!) of things." Mondrian later published a series of essays, *Neo-Plasticism in Pictorial Art*, in 1917–18 to elaborate on his style. As a group of artists *De Stijl* faded after van Doesburg's death in 1931, but its influence lived on in architecture, particularly in the work of the German-born American Ludwig Mies van der Rohe (1886–1969).

Neoplatonism A school of mystical and religious philosophy, developed in the 3rd century AD by the followers of the Egyptian-born Plotinus (c204–270), who considered themselves Platonists ("Neoplatonism" is a modern term) and combined teachings from Plato, Aristotle, Pythagoras and the Stoics with elements of oriental **mysticism** (see **Platonism**). Plotinus taught that there was a hierarchy of spiritual levels through which the individual soul could ascend above the imperfect material world until it merged with the One, from which all existence emanates. The strength of Neoplatonism, which influenced early Christian and Muslim writers and later scholars in the Renaissance, was that it married the rationality of classical Greek thought with the promise of salvation offered by Christianity and by the "mystery" religions of ancient Greece and Rome.

Nepotism The practice by people in authority of favouring their relatives or friends, especially by giving them jobs, often regardless of their suitability or qualifications. Derived from the Latin for "nephew" (*nepos*), the term originates from the habit by which medieval Christian popes and bishops gave preference to their nephews – who in many cases were their illegitimate sons, the priesthood having taken a vow of chastity. The practice was ended in 1692 by Pope Innocent XII (1615–1700 and pope from 1691). However, nepotism has clearly existed throughout history, and continues today, both in business and in politics. In France, President Nicolas Sarkozy was accused of nepotism when his student son, Jean, was elected a local councillor in Neuilly-sur-Seine (a district of which his father was once mayor). In 2009 Jean Sarkozy was in line to become head of the development agency for Paris's La Défense office district – but dropped out in the face of mounting accusations of nepotism.

Nestorianism The doctrine that Jesus Christ was two separate persons, one human and one divine. The term comes from Nestorius (c356–461), the bishop of Constantinople from 428 to 431, who was condemned as a heretic in 431 at the Council of Ephesus, a gathering of the various Christian churches, for this notion and for denouncing the use of the title *Theotokos* – meaning "God-bearer" in Greek – for the Virgin Mary on the grounds that the term undermined the human nature of Jesus Christ. Nestorius argued that while God begot Jesus as God, Mary gave birth to him as a man. The Council of Ephesus (whose findings were confirmed 20 years later by the Council of

Chalcedon), produced the so-called Nestorian schism, with only the Persian church – better known as the Assyrian church – supporting the Nestorian view. The high point of Nestorianism was from the 7th to the 10th centuries, as the church expanded from the Middle East to China and India. In 1551, a number of Nestorians reconciled themselves with the church in Rome and became known as the Chaldeans. After massacres of Nestorians and Chaldeans in the late 19th and early 20th centuries by Kurds and Turks, Nestorianism now survives in small communities in Iraq, Iran, Syria and India and in émigré communities in the Americas.

Nihilism The belief (from the Latin *nihil*, meaning nothing) that existence is without meaning, purpose or value, and so there are no inherent moral values. The Russian author Ivan Turgenev (1818–83) used the term in his 1862 book *Fathers and Sons*, as did the German philosopher Friedrich Nietzsche (1844–1900), who wrote that "a nihilist is a man who judges of the world as it is that it ought not to be, and of the world as it ought to be that it does not exist". In politics, the nihilists were Russian anarchists, originating in the 1860s, whose various groups were associated with violent political action, including the assassination of Tsar Alexander II in 1881. In the arts, nihilism has been connected with Dadaist art and punk music (see Dadaism).

Nominalism The view, from the Latin *nomen*, or "name", that things denominated by a particular term share nothing except that fact. In other words, there are no such things as abstract concepts or "universals" – repeatable entities that can be exemplified by particular things – except as names. Instead, everything that exists is a particular individual. Nominalism was important in medieval thought, in opposition to the doctrine of Platonic realism (which taught that universals have an objective, absolute existence with their own reality). Since realism was associated with religious orthodoxy, nominalism was sometimes considered heretical. The leading proponent of nominalism in the Middle Ages was William of Ockham (1285–1347 or 1349), a British Franciscan friar best known for "Ockham's razor" or the "Law of Parsimony", namely that the simplest explanation of a problem is the best explanation.

Nonconformism See conformism.

Non-interventionism The foreign-policy doctrine that argues that countries may have diplomatic relations with each other but should not interfere in each other's internal affairs. America's first president, George Washington (1732–99), famously declared in his farewell address to the nation in 1796 that "it is our true policy to steer clear of permanent alliances with any portion of the foreign world" – a policy that reflects an enduring isolationist strain in American sentiment (though not in action). But non-interventionism implies neutrality rather than isolation. The leading exponent in modern times is the People's Republic of China, often criticised for making trade deals with unsavoury regimes while being unwilling to press those regimes to change.

Nudism The practice of being naked, for health and lifestyle reasons (as in **naturism**) rather than for sexual motives.

O

Objectivism The practice (akin to objectivity) of emphasising
what is independent of a person's mind. As a
philosophical term, objectivism refers to the belief that
reality exists independently of the mind or human
perception. The Russian-born American writer Ayn Rand
(1905–82), a proponent of objectivism in works such as
The Fountainhead and *Atlas Shrugged*, argued that
"existence is identity; consciousness is identification":
consciousness cannot be conscious of itself, but only of
something beyond itself – in other words, an objective
reality independent of consciousness.

Obscurantism The practice of preventing facts from being
fully known, of preventing enlightenment (the word is
derived from the Latin *obscurans*, or "darkening"). The
idea that knowledge or truth should be kept from the
masses can be traced back to Plato's "noble lie", but the
term comes from the 16th-century satirical *Epistolae
Obscurorum Virorum* (Letters of Obscure Men) in
Germany, which criticised the desire of Dominican
monks to burn Jewish books. Scholars in Europe's

18th-century Age of Enlightenment used the term for religious opposition to the spread of knowledge. Obscurantism is now usually associated with religious **fundamentalism** (as in the phrase "obscurantist clerics"), though there is not necessarily any common link, since fundamentalism implies the preaching of a sincere belief rather than the obscuring of that belief.

Occasionalism A philosophical notion that God is the only cause of an effect – in other words, one finite being or thing does not cause another. The idea originated in medieval Islamic theology, with the Muslim philosopher Al-Ghazali (1058–1111) arguing, for example, that when cotton and fire are put together, it is God, rather than the heat of the flames, that causes the cotton to burn. However, the idea is more usually attributed to a French philosopher, Louis de la Forge (1632–66), a follower of René Descartes, who in his 1665 *Traité de l'esprit de l'homme* (Treatise on the Spirit of Man) developed Descartes's dualist view on the separation of the mind and body (see **dualism**) to explain how this view could be reconciled with the apparent cause-and-effect of thought and action. Occasionalism holds that there is only one true cause, God, who causes effects to appear on the occasions when what seem to be causes appear. If someone strikes a match, God will cause the match to light, with the striking being the "occasional cause" of the lighting.

Oligopolism A rarely used term (from the Greek *oligos*, meaning few and *polein*, meaning sell) for the phenomenon of oligopoly, in which a market is shared by a small number of sellers, so limiting competition. There are various theories for the consequences for consumers: one is that oligopolists will act as a cartel and fix their prices higher than is necessary, perhaps also fixing their production; another is that a single seller will set a lower price to seize an advantage, so forcing others to lower their prices, too; a third theory holds that because rival sellers are more or less forced to follow prices down, but see less advantage, because of a loss of market share, in following prices up, the result is that none will be tempted to change a price and so prices will be stable.

Onanism An old-fashioned term, originating in the early 18th century, for masturbation. A less common meaning is the practice of birth control by *coitus interruptus* (in which the penis is withdrawn before ejaculation). The term refers to the story in the Bible (Genesis 38.8) of Onan, the second son of Judah, who was obliged to marry Tamar, the widow of his elder brother Er. To avoid making Tamar pregnant Onan "spilled his seed" on the ground – a sin for which God killed him.

Optimism The feeling that things will be good, as opposed to pessimism, the feeling that they will be bad. An optimist sees a glass filled halfway as "half full"; a pessimist sees it as "half empty". As a philosophy, optimism is the doctrine promoted by Gottfried Leibniz (1646–1716), a German polymath, who argued that this world is the best of all possible worlds.

Organism A life form, animal or vegetable, existing either as a single cell or as a collection of many cells (billions in the case of human beings). The definition embraces living structures, including fungi and bacteria, that are capable of growth and reproduction, but conventionally excludes bacteria.

Orientalism The study or depiction of eastern cultures by westerners (an orientalist is therefore a scholar engaged in oriental studies). The definition of what is "eastern" varies: art historians have used "orientalism" to refer to 19th-century paintings by French artists in north Africa and the Middle East, but the word can clearly refer to Asia as far as the Pacific. The Palestinian-American scholar Edward Saïd (1935–2003), in his 1978 book *Orientalism*, uses the term to refer to the writings of English, French and American scholars on the Arab world and Islam, criticising them for being overly influenced by the imperialist history of the West. "My contention", he wrote, "is that Orientalism is fundamentally a political doctrine willed over the Orient because the Orient was weaker than the West, which elided the Orient's difference with its weakness."

Orphism A mystical religion, originating in the 7th or 6th century BC in ancient Greece, based on the poems of the mythical Orpheus, who descended into Hades and returned. According to myth, the human race arose from the ashes of the Titans, becoming in part divine (Dionysian) and in part evil (Titanic). Through asceticism and moral purification, an individual would pass through

a series of reincarnations and escape the Titanic
inheritance. Orphism was also the name of a short-lived
art movement, practised around 1912 within the school of
cubism by French artists such as Robert Delaunay
(1885–1941) and Fernand Léger (1881–1955). They preferred
the use of vivid colour to the austere shades of
contemporaries such as Pablo Picasso (1881–1973) and
Georges Braque (1882–1963).

Ostracism The exclusion of a person from a group or a whole
society. The word refers originally to the process in
5th-century Athens by which Athenian citizens could
vote, by scratching a person's name on an *ostrakon*, a
piece of broken pottery, to exile someone from the state
for ten years – on pain of death if they returned earlier.
Nowadays ostracism is rather less severe, in most cases
more akin to cold-shouldering.

p

Pacifism The belief that violence, including war, is never justifiable (pacifism is therefore often synonymous with the refusal of conscientious objectors to participate in military service). Pacifism may be based on pragmatism, with the argument that there must be a less costly way than violence to solve a dispute. More usually it is based on moral principle, with pacifists rejecting the theory, advanced among others by the Roman Catholic church, of the just war. Several Christian denominations, from the Quakers and Anabaptists to the Amish and Jehovah's Witnesses, practise pacifism, citing Christ's command to "turn the other cheek". Perhaps the most famous practitioner of pacifism in modern times (influenced by the pacifist writings of the Russian Leo Tolstoy (1828-1910) in *The Kingdom of God is Within You*) was Mahatma Gandhi (1869-1948), in his campaign of non-violence for India's independence – achieved in 1947 – from Britain.

Paganism The holding of religious beliefs other than the world's main faiths, especially Christianity. The word derives from the Latin *paganus*, meaning rural or villager, with a pagan being synonymous with a heathen (whose origin may be "dwelling on the heath"). Although many pagan festivals have been incorporated into the Christian calendar, pagan and paganism usually carry a disparaging nuance, akin to *kafir* in Islam or gentile in Judaism.

Paleoconservatism The ideology of traditional conservatism, especially in America, with an emphasis on anti-communism and the family and opposition to open immigration (particularly by non-Europeans). The term (the prefix is from the Greek *palaeo*, meaning ancient) was coined in the 1980s to distinguish old-style Republican conservatives from the neoconservative movement that had begun in the 1970s. The neoconservatives, many of whose leading figures were Jewish, were alert to anti-Semitism (often a feature of old-style conservatives) and, unlike the paleoconservatives, advocated an interventionist foreign policy (see interventionism). The split between paleoconservatism and neoconservatism is often traced to the nomination by Ronald Reagan (1911–2004) in 1981 of Mel Bradford, a self-styled traditional conservative from the south, to be chair of the National Endowment for the Humanities. Neoconservatives objected strongly, noting Bradford's criticism of Abraham Lincoln as "a dangerous man".

Pan-Africanism The advocacy of political union for the peoples of Africa, including those in the African diaspora. The origins of pan-Africanism go back to the 18th century and protests against slavery by Africans living in Britain and America, but the first person to use the term "pan-Africanism", as opposed to "the African movement", was Henry Sylvester Williams (1869–1911), a Trinidadian barrister, in organising a conference in London in 1900. A little later the Jamaican Marcus Garvey (1887–1940) emerged as a leader of the movement to "redeem" Africa and expel its colonial powers, saying: "Our union must know no clime, boundary, or nationality. Black men the world over must practise one faith, that of confidence in themselves, with one cause, one goal, one destiny." By the mid-20th century the influence of black Americans and West Indians had given way to indigenous Africans, with the First Conference of Independent African States being held in Ghana in 1958, followed by the founding in 1963 of the Organisation of African Unity, which in 2001–02 was transformed into the African Union. In 2009 the Libyan leader, Muammar Qaddafi, elected chairman of the African Union, declared: "I shall continue to insist that our sovereign countries work to achieve the United States of Africa." Whatever the intentions, the goal of political union seems extremely remote, with Africa's politicians concentrating more realistically on regional economic co-operation.

Pan-Arabism A movement to unite the countries of the Arab world, from Morocco in the west to the Gulf states and Iraq in the east. In emotional terms, pan-Arabism revives memories of the Arab conquests, from Spain to the Indus valley, in the century that followed the death of the Prophet Muhammad in 632. The consequence is an Arab world with a common language, a common religion in

Islam and a sense of shared cultural identity – hence the
stirring of pan-Arabism as early as the 14th century in
opposition to Ottoman rule. During the first world war
(1914–18) Britain and France, seeking Arab allies against
the German-Turkish alliance, encouraged Arab
nationalism (and its tendency to pan-Arabism) under the
Hashemite Sharif Husain bin Ali (1853–1931) of Mecca.
Pan-Arabism, as a secular ideal (many of its exponents
have been Christian rather than Muslim), is fundamental
to **Ba'athism** in Syria and, before the fall of Saddam
Hussein (c1937–2006), in Iraq. It remains a seductive
slogan, but most attempts, notably by the Egyptian
president Gamal Abdul Nasser (1918–70) in the 1950s and
1960s and the Libyan leader Muammar Qaddafi in the
1970s, to unite Arab countries, failed to last. (Qaddafi,
rebuffed in his efforts to forge union with Egypt and
Syria, turned to **pan-Africanism**.) By contrast, the 1990
union of North and South Yemen has survived, as has
the federation in the early 1970s of the seven emirates
that make up the United Arab Emirates.

Panentheism The concept that all is within God – as opposed
to **pantheism**, which holds that all is God. In other words,
in panentheism the universe is part of God, whereas in
pantheism God and the universe are synonymous. The
term panentheism (which comes from the Greek *pan*,
meaning all, *en*, meaning in, and *theos*, meaning god) was
coined by a German philosopher, Karl Krause (1781–1832),
to reconcile the ideas of a god known by faith and of the
world as experienced by the senses (Krause argued that
God was an essence embracing all things, including the

universe). However, the concept has attracted believers among most religions, from Judaism to Hinduism.

Pan-Germanism A movement for the political unification, based on the ties of ethnicity, of all German-speaking peoples, including, for example, those in Alsace, Austria, the Baltic states, Belgium, Luxembourg, Poland and Switzerland. The movement arose from the spirit of European nationalism fomented by the French Revolution in the late 18th century and by the Napoleonic wars of the early 19th century. As the old multi-ethnic monarchies of central and eastern Europe, such as the Romanovs and Hapsburgs, came under threat, German nationalists sought to unite all ethnic Germans. Encouraged by the unification of Germany in 1871, the movement gathered strength until Germany's catastrophic defeat in the first world war. Revival came with the rise of the Nazis, whose pan-Germanism was demonstrated in 1938 with the occupation of the German-speaking Sudetenland in what was then Czechoslovakia. The memory of the Nazi horrors of the second world war has now made the idea of pan-Germanism politically unappealing to both Germans and non-Germans.

Pan-Slavism A movement, originating like pan-Germanism in the nationalist fervour that followed the French Revolution, that aimed to unite the Slavic peoples of central and eastern Europe. The First Pan-Slav Congress took place in Prague in 1848, with a call for equal rights under Austro-Hungarian rule. In Russia pan-Slavism became popular in opposition to the Ottoman empire after Russia's humiliation in the Crimean war of 1853–56, and Slav solidarity was a motive in Russia's support for Serbia against Austria in the crisis that in 1914 sparked the first world war. The collapse of European communism at the end of the 1980s, the division of Czechoslovakia in 1993 into the Czech Republic and Slovakia, and the disintegration in the 1990s of Yugoslavia have now ended most Slavs' dreams of pan-Slavic unity.

Pantheism The belief that all the universe is a manifestation of God ("God is everything and everything is God"), or, more rarely, a belief in all gods. Using the more common definition of the term, which comes from the Greek *pan*, meaning all, and *theos*, meaning god, pantheists – in contrast to theists (see theism) – deny the existence of a personal God transcending, and so separate from, the world. Pantheists and religions such as Christianity are not necessarily mutually exclusive, but religions that are intrinsically pantheistic are Taoism and Hinduism. It has often been argued that the Dutch philosopher Baruch Spinoza (1632–77) was an advocate of pantheism (his ideas led to him being excommunicated by the Jewish community in Amsterdam and to his books being banned by the Roman Catholic church), but some experts consider his ideas amounted rather to panentheism – an etymological nuance meaning that God is both within everything and is also transcendent.

Parallelism The use of two or more similar-sounding words, phrases or clauses in constructing a sentence or speech, usually for rhetorical effect, as in Julius Caesar's "*Veni, vidi, vici*" (I came, I saw, I conquered), or Winston Churchill's "The inherent vice of capitalism is the unequal sharing of blessing; the inherent virtue of socialism is the equal sharing of miseries". Rather more prosaically, parallelism also refers to the use of parallel processing in computer systems.

Parasitism From the Greek *parasitos* – a person eating at another's table – the practice of living off, and so exploiting, others. One example in nature is mistletoe, a leathery-leaved plant growing on oak and other broadleaved trees. Often the relationship is beneficial and symbiotic, as when oxpecker birds pick ticks from the hides of Cape buffalo. Less beneficial is the parasitism of fleas, feeding from the blood of humans and animals.

Pastafarianism Also known as "the Church of the Flying Spaghetti Monster", Pastafarianism was a parody of religion created in 2005 by Bobby Henderson in protest at the decision by the Kansas State Board of Education to require the teaching of intelligent design as an alternative to evolution in the state's public schools. In a satirical letter to the board, describing himself as a "concerned citizen", Henderson wrote: "I think we can all look forward to the time when these three theories are given equal time in our science classrooms across the country, and eventually the world: one third time for Intelligent Design, one third time for Flying Spaghetti Monsterism, and one third time for logical conjecture based on overwhelming observable evidence." Following media publicity, Henderson in 2006 released *The Gospel of the Flying Spaghetti Monster*.

Pastoralism A rural way of life, derived from the Latin *pastor*, or shepherd. More particularly, the word refers to animal husbandry – the raising of livestock. In the Christian church the term refers to the work of the clergy in giving spiritual guidance to their congregation, or "flock".

Paternalism The behaviour of people in authority that limits the freedom of action or responsibility of their subordinates – supposedly in what they feel is the best interest of those subordinates. The term derives from the Latin *pater*, or father, the analogy being that in a family father knows best. The welfare state, with governments providing for the well-being of their citizens, is sometimes said to be an example of state paternalism.

Patriotism A love of one's country, from the Latin *patria*, meaning fatherland, and a zeal to defend it. The term has none of the negative connotations of jingoism or chauvinism (or even, in some contexts, nationalism), though it should be remembered that the British author and lexicographer Dr Samuel Johnson (1709–84) bitingly declared that "patriotism is the last refuge of a scoundrel" in a reference to the demagogic British politician John Wilkes (1725–97).

Pauperism The condition, from the Latin *pauper*, meaning poor, of being stricken by destitution and so dependent on charity or government aid. "Pauper" originated in

English in the late 15th century in the Latin legal phrase *in forma pauperis* (in the form of a poor person), which allowed the waiving of court costs.

Pelagianism A 5th-century heretical Christian doctrine taught by Pelagius (c354–420), a monk born probably in either Britain or Ireland. Pelagius, disturbed by the lax morality he found among fellow Christians, rejected the argument that they sinned because of human weakness. Instead, he argued that God made humans free to choose between good and evil, and so sin was voluntary. He and his disciple, Celestius, denied the Catholic church's doctrine of original sin and the necessity of infant baptism. Pelagianism was opposed by Augustine (354–430), bishop of Hippo (also known as St Augustine), who argued that humans could attain righteousness only through the grace of God. Pelagius and Celestius were both excommunicated in 418, but their teaching – that moral perfection is attainable through free will – was preached openly in southern Italy until the death in 455 of the movement's then leader, Julian, bishop of Eclanum.

Pentecostalism A fundamentalist (see fundamentalism) Christian movement, originating in America in the late 19th century from the Holiness movement, in which believers would experience the intercession of the Holy Spirit. The origin of the word is from the Greek *pentecoste* (*hemera*), meaning fiftieth (day), a reference to the Christian Whitsunday, falling on the 50th day after Easter, and to the Jewish festival of Shavuot, held on the 50th day after the second day of Passover. Pentecostalists are prone to "speak in tongues" – unintelligible utterances delivered in a kind of ecstatic trance – during their services, in accordance with the account in the Bible, Acts 2:1–4, of how the Holy Spirit on the 50th day after Passover descended on the first Christians, enabling them to "speak in other tongues". There are today many Pentecostal denominations, with collectively perhaps 110m adherents. Though the origins of the movement lie in America, Pentecostalism has become increasingly popular in developing countries in Africa and Asia.

Perfectionism The refusal to accept anything that is less than perfect. As a personality trait, perfectionism is sometimes considered an unhealthy refusal to accept reality. As the Spanish artist Salvador Dali (1904–89) once said, "Have no fear of perfection – you'll never reach it."

Peronism A political and economic ideology based on the populist ideas of Juan Domingo Perón (1895–1974), president of Argentina from 1946 to 1955 and again from October 1973 to July 1974. Peronism, which is also known in Spanish as *justicialismo* (social justice), emphasises both nationalism and statism, with the government subsidising business and industry. To many critics, Peronism is close to fascism (Perón spent 18 years in exile in Franco's Spain and was an avowed admirer of Benito Mussolini), is stained by the human-rights abuses in Argentina under several Peronist governments and is economically incompetent. Although at one time Peronism embraced the political left and right, in the early 1970s Peronism became aggressively (and murderously) anti-left and anti-Marxist. In Argentina today Peronism remains a political force through the Partido Justicialista, the party of former presidents Carlos Menem and Eduardo Duhalde and subsequently of Néstor Kirchner, president from 2003 to 2007, and then of his wife and successor, Cristina Fernández Kirchner.

Pessimism The tendency to see or expect the worst. While an optimist sees a glass filled halfway as half full (see **optimism**), a pessimist sees it as half empty. In philosophy, pessimism is the belief that the world is as bad as can be, and that evil will prevail over good.

Phalangism An alternative spelling of **Falangism**, used particularly for the ideology of the right-wing Lebanese Christian Maronite Phalange party (officially called the Lebanese Social Democratic Party), founded by Pierre Gemayel (1905–84) in 1936. In this sense, phalangism is the espousal of Lebanese **nationalism** (the party's motto is "God, Nation and Family"), first against French colonial rule and then, after Lebanon's independence in 1943, against what the party saw as the influence of neighbouring Muslim states and the increasing presence within Lebanon of Palestinian refugees. In Arabic the Phalangists are called *kata'ib*, plural of *katiba* and the translation of the Latin and Greek *phalanx*, meaning infantry formation. They were the dominant Christian force in the Lebanese civil war of 1975–90.

Phallocentrism The notion of male dominance, through a
symbolic focus on the phallus or penis. The word was a
neologism coined by the deconstructionist French
philosopher Jacques Derrida (1930–2004), who also used,
with an identical meaning, the word "phallogocentrism".

Pharisaism The doctrine of the Pharisees, a Jewish sect that
first appeared in history in the 2nd century BC. The
Pharisees (the term is derived from a Hebrew word
meaning set apart) believed there were two Torahs (the
law of God as revealed to Moses): both the written Torah
of five books and an "oral Torah", which encompassed
not just an oral revelation to Moses but also the product
of rabbinical debate. This allowed Jews to interpret the
law of Moses in the light of changing circumstances (for
example, colonisation by the Romans), but it also meant
that there was a Pharisaic ruling for virtually every
feature of life, leading to the accusation that the Pharisees
were more interested in the letter of the law than its
spirit. The main opponents of the Pharisees were the
Sadducees, who believed only in the written Torah. In
contrast to the Sadducees, the Pharisees believed in an
afterlife and the resurrection of the dead. After the
destruction of the temple in Jerusalem in 70AD, the
Pharisees disappeared from history, but their theology
has remained influential among rabbinical scholars (by
contrast, Christian tradition has a low regard for the
Pharisees, accusing them of hypocrisy – though Jesus was
possibly a Pharisee and St Paul certainly was).

Phenomenalism A philosophical theory that knowledge is
confined to what is perceived by the senses. In the words
of the British philosopher John Stuart Mill (1806–73),
"Objects are the permanent possibilities of sensation."
The theory can be traced back to George Berkeley
(1685–1753), an Anglo-Irish philosopher, and David Hume
(1711–76), a Scottish philosopher. Hume argued that
percepts (what is perceived) and concepts are the sole
objects of knowledge, with the objects of perception and
the nature of the mind itself remaining unknowable.
Physical objects do not exist as things in themselves but
only as sensory perceptions (for example, redness or
hardness) situated in time and in space. The term
"matter" is meaningless for phenomenalists unless
defined by reference to sensations. In the "bundle theory"
of phenomenalism, objects consist of bundles of
perceptions: an apple can be perceived as being green
and hard – and when the greenness and hardness are no
longer perceived, the apple no longer exists. But what if
the apple is in an empty room? The solution is to
construct a hypothesis: "If there were someone in the
room, he or she would perceive the apple." (See also
sensationalism.)

Photojournalism The practice of transmitting news in
newspapers and magazines by photographs. The origins
of photojournalism lie in pictures taken of the Crimean
war in the mid-19th century, but the "golden age" was in
the mid-20th century, when magazines such as *Life* in
America and *Paris Match* in France built large circulations
through their use of photographs. Magnum Photos, a

co-operative agency established in 1947 by Henri Cartier-Bresson (1908–2004) and Robert Capa (1913–54), among others, has become a byword for superb coverage of world events and cultural phenomena by some of the world's best photographers. At the same time, the development of digital photography, enabling even a mobile phone to take photographs, has in the 21st century created a new breed of "citizen photojournalists", encouraged by news outlets to send them their photographs.

Pietism The state of being, perhaps excessively, devoutly religious. In history, Pietism was a religious movement, begun in Germany in the 1670s and lasting until the mid-18th century, for the revival of piety (from the Latin *pietas*) in the Lutheran church. Its first leader was Philipp Jakob Spener (1635–1705), who published *Pia Desideria* (Pious Desires) in 1675. These goals were greater private and public use of the Scriptures; greater involvement of the laity; the importance of testifying to the practical benefits of living faith; ministerial training that emphasised piety rather than scholasticism; and preaching with the purpose of instruction. As part of this, Spener organised *collegiae pietatis* (assemblies of piety) in which lay Christians would meet for Bible study and religious discussion. After Spener, leadership of the movement passed to August Hermann Francke (1663–1727), who made the university of Halle a centre of Pietism (Heinrich Melchior Mühlenberg was sent from Halle in 1742 to organise American Lutheranism). Pietism

survives in parts of Germany and is implicit in
evangelical **Protestantism** around the world.

Plagiarism Taking someone else's writing or ideas and
passing them off as one's own. The word, derived from
the Latin *plagiarius*, or kidnapper, was first used in the
early 17th century but undoubtedly, human nature being
what it is, instances of plagiarism long predate that.
Accusations, proven or not, of plagiarism have frequently
featured in academic writing, journalism and music. In
the 1970s, for example, the former Beatle George Harrison
was successfully sued for copying the melody of the
Chiffons' *He's So Fine* for his own song *My Sweet Lord*.
Plagiarism in music may often be unintentional. This is
less likely in scientific writing, literature and journalism.
In 2009 the British poet Andrew Motion was accused of
"shameless burglary" by a military historian, Ben
Shephard, after using passages from a book by Shephard.
Motion replied that Shephard had "got the wrong end of
the stick" and that his use of lines from Shephard's book
was an example of "found poetry" going back to
Shakespeare. In the age of Google, plagiarism has become
both easier to commit and easier to detect – as many a
student and teacher has realised.

Platonism The philosophy of Plato (c428–347BC) and his
followers, arguing in the "theory of forms" that there
exist abstract objects of which objects that can be
identified by the senses are imperfect copies. Based on
the teachings of Plato's master, Socrates, Platonism
appears to deny the reality of the material world. In

Plato's "allegory of the cave", Socrates reckons the invisible world to be the most knowable and the visible world the least knowable. The idea is that prisoners in a cave who can only see shadows on the wall of the cave attribute forms to these shadows, which is the closest they can get to seeing reality. By contrast, the philosopher is like a prisoner freed from the cave and able to see that the shadows are not reality.

Pluralism A state in which two or more coexist, hence in politics the idea of sharing power among a number of parties or holding more than one office at the same time. In philosophy, pluralism is the recognition of more than one principle; in religion, pluralism holds that no one religion is the sole source of truth.

Plutonism The theory, first put forward by the Scottish geologist James Hutton (1726–97), that igneous rocks such as granite were formed by the solidification of molten magma beneath the Earth's surface. Plutonism (named after Pluto, the Roman god of the underworld) supplanted the "Neptunism" (from Neptune, the Roman god of the sea) theory of the German geologist Abraham Werner (1750–1817), who held that rocks were sedimentary in origin, the result of a great flood.

Pointillism A style of neo-Impressionist painting in the 19th century in which the artist uses tiny dots of primary colours which blend together in the viewer's eye to form shapes and the impression of secondary colours. The artist most associated with pointillism was Georges-Pierre

Seurat (1859–91). An example is his painting *A Sunday Afternoon on the Island of La Grande Jatte*. Ironically, the term pointillism – coined by art critics in the 1880s – was first used to ridicule the style.

Polymorphism The state of having many shapes or forms. In biology, for example, polymorphism (from the Greek *polu-*, meaning many, and *morphe*, meaning form) means the occurrence of different forms within a single population or within the life cycle of an organism. In computing, polymorphism is a feature of a programming language allowing different data types to be handled by a uniform interface.

Polytheism The belief in more than one god, as opposed to monotheism, the belief in a single god. Polytheism, from the Greek *polu-*, meaning many, and *theos*, meaning god, was a feature of Pharaonic Egypt and of ancient Greece and Rome, with the various gods and goddesses gathered in a "pantheon". It remains a feature of several religions, such as Hinduism and Shintoism (though many Hindus consider that their faith's various deities emanate from a single god).

Populism The practice of appealing to the people, as opposed to any elite. In politics, populism can come close to demagoguery, and is often associated with fascism, nationalism and the extreme right. Nonetheless, any political party, regardless of its place on the ideological spectrum, is likely to advance a populist policy or initiative to win votes.

Positivism The quality of being positive, as opposed to
negative. As a school of philosophy positivism, a term
first used in the 19th century by the French philosopher
Auguste Comte (1798-1857), maintains that every rational
assertion can be verified by science, logic or mathematics.
In other words, the only true knowledge is that which is
based on experience, to the exclusion of metaphysical
speculation. Positivism, also espoused by John Stuart Mill
(1806-73), is closely related to empiricism and
pragmatism. **Logical positivism** was a development
formulated by the Vienna Circle of philosophers in the
1920s. They argued that knowledge depended on the
verification of public rather than personal experience,
and considered that metaphysical doctrines were not so
much false as meaningless.

Postcolonialism An approach to politics, literature and
sociology, originating in the second half of the 20th
century, that is based in or deals with the experiences of
former colonies. Notable theorists of postcolonialism
were the French writer Frantz Fanon (1925-61) and the
Palestinian-American Edward Saïd (1935-2003). Fanon,
whose opposition to colonialism led him from theory to
action, working to help Algerian resistance fighters (he
was himself wounded in 1957 near the Algerian-Tunisian
border), wrote the influential *Les Damnés de la terre* (The
Wretched of the Earth) in 1961, calling for the
dispossessed peoples of the world to rise up in violent
revolution. Intrinsic to postcolonialism is the difficult
legacy of **colonialism** in many countries: witness the
problem of forming a national identity, for example,

when frontiers left by the colonisers pay scant regard to ethnicity, language or religion (as in Nigeria).

Postmodernism A late 20th-century concept in philosophy, the arts and architecture that mistrusts the grand theories associated with **modernism** and argues that there is no absolute truth. Postmodernism, in many ways a disillusioned reaction to the second world war, has no central organising principle and has therefore often been the subject of parody. A leading theorist of postmodernism was the French sociologist Jean Baudrillard (1929–2007). In art, postmodernism embraces installation art and "happenings". In architecture, postmodernism rejects the stark functionality of modernism and attempts to add an element of beauty. The modernist architect Mies van der Rohe (1886–1969) famously said: "Less is more." The postmodernist Robert Venturi has countered: "Less is a bore."

Poststructuralism A movement, associated with **postmodernism** and created by French intellectuals in the politically and socially turbulent late 1960s, that mistrusts the pretensions to objectivity of **structuralism**. Instead, poststructuralism holds that language is a code, with its meaning derived from the contrast of its various parts. Key proponents of poststructuralism included Jacques Derrida (1930–2004) and Roland Barthes (1915–80). In literary criticism, poststructuralists reject the idea of a text having a single meaning imposed by the author. Instead, every reader creates a new meaning. Ironically, many poststructuralists, such as Barthes and Michel Foucault

(1926–84), were formerly – or even simultaneously
– structuralists.

Pragmatism Derived from the Greek for "deed", pragmatism
is an attitude or form of behaviour that focuses on
practicality. Therefore, in philosophy, pragmatism is a
movement that accepts a proposition if it is seen to work.
The philosophical movement began in 19th-century
America with the ideas of William James (1842–1910),
John Dewey (1859–1952) and Charles Sanders Peirce
(1839–1914). Peirce later called these ideas "pragmaticism"
– a name "ugly enough to be safe from kidnappers"
(though he argued that his ideas were not quite the same
as James's). In contrast to Cartesians and their quest for
certainty, pragmatists believe no statement about the
world is absolutely certain; instead, theories may need to
be modified in the light of experience.

Presbyterianism A form of government in Protestant
Christianity in which the church is administered locally
by a pastor and a group of elders (*presbyteros* is Greek for
elder) for each congregation and then regionally and
nationally by courts composed of ministers and elders.
This form of government was introduced by John Calvin
in Geneva in 1541, on the basis that it represented the
practice of the early church.

Presentism The practice of interpreting the past according to
the attitudes and values of the present – a temptation to
which politicians, journalists and even historians are
wont to succumb.

Priapism A condition in which a man's penis is persistently, and often painfully, erect. The word comes from the Greek *priapizein*, meaning "to be lewd", and is a reference to Priapus, the god of fertility in Greek mythology, whose penis was pictured as disproportionately large and erect.

Prism A geometric figure, from the Greek *prisma*, meaning a "thing sawn", with two end faces that are equal and with sides that are parallelograms. In optics, a prism is therefore a triangular device that can separate white light into a spectrum of colours. Used figuratively, the term implies distortion: for example, black Americans might well view politics through the prism of racism.

Progressivism The favouring of change and reform in society and politics, usually – though not invariably – associated with parties of the political left. In America, progressivism made its mark in the late 19th century onwards as a reaction to, and remedy for, the social problems brought about by industrialisation and urbanisation. Cities such as Toledo, Detroit and San Francisco, for example, elected progressive mayors in the 1890s who promised municipal ownership of utilities and better housing codes. President Theodore Roosevelt (1858–1919), though a Republican, was also a leader of the Progressive Movement, taking measures in the first years of the 20th century to regulate the railways and break up monopolies.

Proselytism The seeking of converts to a religion – a corollary of evangelical Christianity (see evangelism) and a duty of the Mormons (see **Mormonism**), who normally spend a period of their youth as missionaries. While Christianity in general feels a need to "spread the word of God", there are many religions that eschew proselytism. **Judaism**, for example, traditionally seeks no converts, and religious membership for the Druzes and most Zoroastrians (see **Zoroastrianism**) can only be inherited, not acquired. The derivation of the word is from the Greek *proseluthos*, meaning stranger or convert, which in turn comes from *proserkhesthai*, meaning approach.

Protectionism The practice of protecting a country's domestic industries or companies from foreign competition by restricting imports, usually by quotas or tariffs (though also by non-tariff barriers such as managed exchange rates or excessive paperwork). Most economists, citing the "law of comparative advantage" outlined by David Ricardo (1772–1823) in 1817, agree that protectionism makes little sense when contrasted with the benefits of free trade. Nonetheless, protectionism has been politically tempting throughout history, be it during the mercantilist period of empire building or the more modern focus on minimising unemployment. Protectionists cite the need to safeguard sectors, such as agriculture, when foreign sources might be cut off in time of war; the need to protect "key" industries such as defence; and the need to protect jobs. In developing countries, it is often argued that infant companies and industries need a period of protection so that they can grow strong enough to survive international competition. All these arguments have a certain force, but all too often they result in harmful distortions or delay inevitable economic adjustment. For example, the European Union's protectionist subsidies to farmers through its Common Agricultural Policy have certainly made Europe self-sufficient in food – but at an enormous cost that could have been better spent elsewhere, and also to the detriment of farmers in developing countries who have to compete with EU surpluses dumped on the world market. In pointing out the dangers of protectionism, free traders note the damaging impact of America's imposition of import tariffs during the Great Depression, with world trade falling by 66% between 1929 and 1934.

Protestantism One of the three main branches of Christianity, the other two being **Roman Catholicism** and the Eastern Orthodox church. Protestantism originated in the 16th-century Reformation in which European theologians such as Martin Luther (1483–1546) sought (and failed) to reform the Roman Catholic church. The first use of the word was in 1529, when the Lutheran minority in the Catholic-dominated Diet of Speyer, in Germany, objected to the decision that the authority of the Catholic church be restored and issued a formal "protestation" that "in matters which concern God's honour and salvation and the eternal life of our souls, everyone must stand and give account before God for himself". Protestantism is not so much a denomination of Christianity as a collection of denominations, from Anglicans to Anabaptists, which all reject papal authority and accept just two sacraments – **baptism** and communion – rather than the seven of the Roman

Catholics (baptism, communion or Eucharist, reconciliation or penance, confirmation, marriage, holy orders and the anointing of the sick). Protestants also hold that forgiveness comes through faith alone; that the priesthood is for all believers; and that the Holy Scriptures are the supreme authority. However, in matters of liturgy the Anglicans are extremely close to the Roman Catholics, whereas Baptists, for example, retain very little of Catholic ritual.

Puritanism A censorious attitude towards pleasure, especially sexual pleasure. In religion, Puritanism was a reform movement in the late 16th and 17th centuries among British Protestants who regarded the Reformation of the Church of England under Elizabeth I (1533–1603, reigning from 1558) as unfinished, and who wanted to "purify" **Anglicanism** from the remnants of Roman Catholic "popery". The Reformation, that is the separation from Roman Catholic authority, had occurred in 1534 in the reign of the much-married Henry VIII and **Protestantism** had continued under Edward VI – but during the reign of Queen Mary (1553–58) England had returned to **Roman Catholicism**, before reverting again to Protestantism on the accession of Elizabeth. During the reign of Elizabeth's successor, James I (James VI of Scotland), the Puritans suffered persecution, which encouraged the first Puritan emigration to America on the Mayflower in 1620. Some Puritans had earlier chosen to remain in the Church of England; they became known, after the restoration of the monarchy in 1660 (following the interlude of Cromwell's rule), as Nonconformists for their refusal to conform to the Book of Common Prayer (others became "Separatists", leaving the Anglican church altogether). In their doctrine, the Puritans adhered to Calvinism: for example, God had decided before the creation of the world who was damned and who would be saved; Christ died for the select only; and man was born in sin. The Puritan "great migration" to America in the 1630s has indelibly influenced the culture of the country, not just with the growth of fundamentalist and evangelical Christianity but also with strict attitudes towards moral laxity and alcohol (witness the period of Prohibition from 1920 to 1933).

q

Quakerism The doctrine of the Religious Society of Friends, a
Christian movement of some 210,000 followers founded
around 1650 by George Fox (1624–91), a British "dissenter"
from the Church of England. The Quakers, or Friends,
believe each person has an "inner light", with God
working directly with the soul. In consequence, there is
no need for any intermediary, such as a priest. The
Quakers originally saw themselves as returning to the
purity of early Christianity, and as such often called each
other "saint". In contrast to other Christian
denominations, there is no set liturgy; nor do Quakers
practice **baptism** or celebrate the Eucharist. Quakers
gather in Meeting Houses rather than churches, and stay
silent until "moved by the spirit" to say something to the
meeting. So different are Quaker beliefs from the
mainstream of Christianity that in the early years they
frequently faced persecution as heretics. In the
Massachusetts Bay colony in America, for example,
Quakers were exiled on pain of death; and in Britain they
were banned from sitting in Parliament from 1698 to 1833.
However, the American state of Pennsylvania was
founded in 1681 by William Penn (1644–1718), a Quaker

contemporary of Fox, as a community based on Quaker **pacifism**. The name "Quaker" may allude to the apparent fits experienced by worshippers when moved by the Holy Spirit, but is more likely to come from Fox's journal, recounting that in his court appearance in 1650 on a charge of blasphemy, Justice Bennet "called us Quakers because we bid them tremble at the word of God". One characteristic of the Quaker movement is its philanthropy and sense of social justice, illustrated, for example, by the way that the Cadbury family in 19th- and 20th-century Britain established the "model village" of Bournville for the workers in its chocolate factory.

Quietism An acceptance of things as they are, but more particularly in Christianity a mystical recourse to meditation and the abandonment of the will. The term originated with the teachings of the Spanish priest Miguel de Molinos (c1628–96), whose doctrines, paying scant attention to Catholic ritual and authority, were condemned as heresy by Pope Innocent XI in 1687.

Quixotism The quality of being quixotic – that is, being idealistic at the expense of being practical and of seeking fanciful and unrealisable goals, especially romantic and chivalrous ones. The word, first used in the late 18th century, is an allusion to the naively romantic Don Quixote in the two volumes, published in 1605 and 1615, of the satirical novel *The Ingenious Hidalgo Don Quixote de la Mancha*, by the Spanish writer Miguel de Cervantes (1547–1616). By "tilting at windmills", or attacking imaginary enemies, Don Quixote was indulging in quixotism.

r

Racialism Another, less common, word for racism.

Racism The belief that races are not equal, and so the practice
of prejudice and discrimination against someone of a
different, supposedly inferior race. Racism has
undoubtedly existed throughout history: the ancient
Greeks and Romans called foreigners "barbarians", a
word with a pejorative nuance. Racism towards the
natives of their colonies was a common feature of
European imperialism and an obvious component of
slavery in America (whose black population still suffers
from acts of racism despite equal-opportunity legislation).
It also underlay Adolf Hitler's notion of Aryan supremacy
and the Nazis' persecution of the Jews. One of the
clearest practices of racism in more modern times was
the system of apartheid, or segregation, in South Africa
from 1948 to 1991, with whites considered superior to
their "coloured" (or mixed race) and black compatriots.
Stokely Carmichael (1941–98), a Black Panther and black
civil-rights activist in 1960s America, is credited with
coining the term "institutional racism", for racism

committed by governments, public bodies or corporations. A 1999 report by a committee inquiring into the 1993 murder of a black youngster in London accused the Metropolitan Police of "institutional racism" – and the police accepted the charge.

Radicalism The practice (from *radix*, the Latin for root) of going back to fundamentals. In politics, radicalism is the practice of promoting fundamental change in society and is often associated with parties of the left. Historically, the term was first used in 18th-century Britain and became more common in the 19th century, notably to describe the electoral reform ideas of the Liberal Party. It was also a political theme in 19th-century France, where Georges Clemenceau's Radicals claimed to be the heirs of the French Revolution. Today, the word is often used in the term "Islamic radicalism", more or less synonymous with Islamic **fundamentalism**.

Randianism The philosophy of the Russian-born American writer Ayn Rand (1905–82) and her embrace of **objectivism**, a philosophy that extols laissez-faire capitalism and the power of the individual. Rand, born Alissa Zinovievna Rosenbaum, wrote, among other works, two best-selling novels to articulate the notion that achievement comes from individual effort. In *The Fountainhead*, published in 1943, the protagonist maintains his integrity against the temptation to compromise; in *Atlas Shrugged*, published in 1957, two industrialists struggle to continue their business as society decays. Contained in Rand's writing is always the struggle

of the individual against collectivism, a theme that struck
a popular chord in America in the second half of the
20th century.

Rastafarianism A religious movement, originating in Jamaica
in the 1930s, that holds that Haile Selassie (1892–1975),
emperor of Ethiopia from 1930 to 1974, was the Messiah,
who would lead Africans and people of African origin to
a golden age. The word derives from *ras*, meaning head
and a title of nobility in Ethiopia, and *tafari*, part of Haile
Selassie's pre-coronation name. Rastafarians are
monotheists (see monotheism), calling God "Jah", who
lives within each person – hence the way Rastafarians
often refer to themselves as "I and I", which can also be
used for "we". Jesus, considered by Rastafarians to be
black, is accepted as a personification of God. His
teachings, however, have been corrupted by "Babylon",
or white, western society. By contrast, Zion, the land
promised by Jah, is Africa, particularly Ethiopia. The
smoking of ganja, or cannabis, is a spiritual act essential
to Rastafarianism. Some Rastafarians consider that
wearing their hair in matted dreadlocks is also essential
to their faith.

Rationalism The belief that opinions and actions should be
based on reason, as opposed to emotion or religious faith.
As a philosophical theory rationalism – in contrast to
empiricism – holds that reason, not experience, is the
basis and test of knowledge. Rationalism was intrinsic to
the thinking in the 17th century of René Descartes
(1596–1650), who argued that mathematical truths could

only be arrived at by reason. Other 17th-century exponents of rationalism were the German philosopher Gottfried Leibniz (1646–1716) and the Dutch philosopher Baruch Spinoza (1632–77).

Reaganism The political and social philosophy of Ronald Reagan (1911–2004), America's president from 1981 to 1989, characterised by the belief that government intervention is invariably bad (government should therefore be as small as possible). Accompanying this belief was an advocacy of **monetarism** and supply-side economics and a foreign policy based on a strong military and opposition to **communism** and the Soviet Union ("the evil empire", in Reagan's phrase). Reaganism in America was matched in the 1980s in its free-trade convictions and supply-side economics by **Thatcherism** in Britain. Supply-side economics holds that an artificial increase in aggregate demand (for example, by Keynesian intervention) achieves nothing in real terms since more labour will be needed to meet the increase in demand and this will require an increase in wages. Instead, improvements to the supply of labour and goods should be made by measures such as cutting taxes, eliminating monopolies, reducing regulation, limiting the anti-competitive activity of trade unions and increasing the mobility of labour. Both Reagan and Thatcher were heavily influenced by neoconservative thinkers and by monetarist economists, such as Milton Friedman (1912–2006), from the University of Chicago.

Realism The practice of accepting reality, and so of dealing with things as they are. Realism in art and literature involves accurate depiction, even at the expense of beauty, for example in the 19th-century paintings of Gustave Courbet (1819–77) and the novels of Honoré de Balzac (1799–1850), Stendhal (1783–1842) and Gustave Flaubert (1821–80). As a philosophical term, realism goes back to ancient Greece and Plato's concept of "universals" – properties that can apply to many things rather than just one. Realism holds that universals really do exist (by contrast, conceptualism holds that they exist only in the mind).

Reductionism The practice of simplifying a complex phenomenon so that it becomes more easily intelligible – in other words, reducing the complicated to its underlying fundamentals. The seductive argument is that a complex system is simply the sum of its parts, and the parts can be – reductively – studied individually.

Regalism The doctrine of royal supremacy or prerogative, especially in the affairs of the church. Regalism was a feature of Gallicanism, the doctrine developed in medieval France that subordinated the rights of the church to the power of the state.

Regionalism The practice of political or economic administration at the regional rather than central or local level. As a linguistic term, regionalism refers to a feature of language, such as pronunciation or the choice of words, specific to a particular region. In geopolitics, regionalism refers to political or economic collaboration – such as the Association of South-East Asian Nations or the North American Free Trade Agreement – concluded on a regional rather than global basis.

Relativism The idea that concepts such as truth and morality are not absolute but exist in relation to their context. A clichéd example is that "beauty is in the eye of the beholder". Relativism is hardly new: the 5th-century BC Greek historian Herodotus noted that each society thinks its way of doing things is the best, and in the 17th century Baruch Spinoza (1632–77) argued that nothing is intrinsically good or evil (a view disputed by many today, who argue that genocide, for example, is inherently evil).

Republicanism The advocacy of a republic – as opposed to, say, a hereditary monarchy – as the proper form of government. The term derives from the Latin *res publica* (meaning public matter) and was originally applied to the form of government common to classical Athens and Sparta and to pre-imperial Rome. The underlying principle of republicanism is that it gives the individual citizen a stake in the common good. In modern usage (at least outside Britain and much of the Commonwealth, whose symbolic head is the British monarch), republicanism tends to mean the ideology of the Republican Party in the United States. It can also be qualified, so that Irish republicanism, for example, means the ambition for some, mainly Catholic, in Northern Ireland to unite this part of the United Kingdom (a monarchy) with the Republic of Ireland. Similarly, in

Australia republicanism means the desire to remove the British monarch as its head of state.

Revisionism A term, often derogatory, to describe the modification or reinterpretation of historical events or of a political ideology. For example, the reinterpretation of Marxism to argue that violent revolution is not a necessary precursor to socialism, which, instead, can be achieved through evolution.

Rightism Support for the views and policies of the political right.

Roman Catholicism The practices and doctrines of the Roman Catholic church, the largest Christian denomination with over 1 billion followers. Roman Catholicism is characterised by the authority it grants to its head, the pope, as the successor to the Apostle St Peter – notably in the doctrine, defined in 1870, of papal infallibility. Other features include the celebration of the mass or Eucharist, in which, according to the doctrine of transubstantiation, the consecrated bread and wine become the body and blood of Christ; the veneration of the Virgin Mary, as the mother of Jesus, and of other saints; the celibacy of the priesthood; the practice of confession by believers to be absolved of their sins; and opposition to contraception and abortion. Much of the ritual and thinking of Roman Catholicism came as a response by the church's ecumenical Council of Trent (1545–63) to the attempts by Martin Luther (1483–1546), beginning in 1517, to reform the church. Those attempts led to the Protestant Reformation and the schism between the Roman Catholic church and the Protestants (see **Protestantism**).

Romanticism   The state of being romantic. In the arts, romanticism was a movement originating in the late 18th century that emphasised subjective inspiration and the exalted individual as a reaction against the constraints of **neoclassicism** and the **rationalism** of the Enlightenment. The movement included painters such as J.M.W. Turner (1775–1851) and Eugène Delacroix (1798–1863). In painting, romanticism gave way to **realism** in the 1840s, but in music, romanticism continued throughout the 19th century, with composers such as Franz Schubert (1797–1828) and Franz Liszt (1811–86). In literature, romanticism included poets such as Lord Byron (1788–1824) and Percy Bysshe Shelley (1792–1822) and writers such as Aleksandr Pushkin (1799–1837).

Rosicrucianism   The practices of the Rosicrucians, a secret order in the 17th and 18th centuries devoted to **mysticism** and aspiring to alchemy. The society was supposedly formed after the publication of an anonymous pamphlet in 1614 featuring a mythical 15th-century German knight called Christian Rosenkreuz (literally "rose cross" – a combination that gave the order its symbol). Some accounts say that Rosenkreuz was really Paracelsus, a 16th-century Swiss physician and alchemist; others that he was really the English philosopher Francis Bacon (1561–1626). In any event, Rosenkreuz is said to have brought back to Europe wisdom and knowledge acquired from Sufis and Zoroastrians on trips to the Middle East.

Several groups today use the term to describe themselves, stressing mysticism rather than any particular religious doctrine.

S

Sabbatarianism The observance of the Sabbath – the seventh day of the week – by Jews between Friday evening and Saturday evening and by Christians on Sunday (though some Christian sabbatarians observe the Jewish Sabbath). The origins of the term, derived from the Hebrew *shabbath*, meaning rest, lie in the Biblical account of creation in the book of Genesis, where God created the heavens and the Earth in six days and then rested on the seventh. For Christians, observance of the Sabbath as a day of rest constitutes the fourth ("Remember the Sabbath Day, to keep it Holy") of the Bible's Ten Commandments. The idea is also rooted in the notion that Christ was resurrected on the first day of the week. Sabbatarianism was strictly enforced by British Presbyterians in the 17th century, especially during the so-called interregnum between the abolition of the monarchy in 1649 and the restoration of Charles II in 1660.

Sacerdotalism The system or practices of the priesthood (from the Latin *sacerdos*, or priest, meaning "one who gives a sacred offering"). In particular the term refers to a doctrine attributing supernatural powers to priests or the right to make a propitiatory sacrifice. In **Roman Catholicism**, according to Vatican II (the conclusions of an ecumenical council of the Vatican in 1962–65 under Pope John XXXIII and Pope Paul VI), "through the ministry of priests, the spiritual sacrifice of the faithful is made perfect in union with the [eternal] sacrifice of Christ, the sole Mediator. Through the hands of the priests and in the name of the whole Church, the Lord's sacrifice is offered in the Eucharist [Holy Communion] in an unbloody and sacramental manner until He Himself returns." By contrast, Lutherans reject sacerdotalism, arguing that the Eucharist is not a sacrifice by priests to protect congregants from divine wrath but is offered by God as an assurance of his mercy (see **Lutheranism**).

Sadism The derivation of pleasure, especially sexual pleasure, from inflicting pain and humiliation on others. If the recipients accept their pain and humiliation willingly, they are masochists (see **masochism**), and the shared practice is known as sadomasochism. The term was coined in the late 19th century by Richard von Krafft-Ebing (1840–1902), a German psychiatrist, referring to the Marquis de Sade (1740–1814), a French aristocrat who chronicled his perverted sexual practices in a series of erotic novels and advocated licentiousness unrestrained by conventional morality.

Salafism A movement in Sunni Islam that seeks to restore religious purity by hearkening back to the early days of

Islam. Salafism is often used interchangeably with **Wahhabism** (the dominant school of Islam in Saudi Arabia and Qatar), since the preaching in the 18th century of Muhammad ibn Abd al-Wahhab (1703–92) called for a return to the religious practices of the first three generations of Muslims. The word comes from the Arabic *salaf*, meaning predecessor or forefather, with Salafis admiring the early generations of Muslims. In the 19th century in Egypt Muhammad Abduh (1849–1905) and Jamal al-Din al-Afghani (1838–97) used the word "Salafi" to describe their movement for an Islamic revival. In the late 20th century and now in the 21st century Salafism has been associated by western observers with violence and often **terrorism**, with the French scholar Gilles Kepel coining the term "Salafist-**jihadism**" to describe the activities of Salafist Muslims in combating the regime in Algeria, or Soviet and later NATO troops in Afghanistan.

Sapphism A synonym for **lesbianism**, coined in the late 19th century from the name of Sappho (c620–570BC), a Greek poetess born on the island of Lesbos, whose poems, perhaps autobiographical, often speak of love for women (in the late 18th century there are references in English writings to "Sapphic passion", "Sapphic lovers" and "Sapphists").

Satanism The worship of Satan, or the devil in Abrahamic religions (Satan, in its original Hebrew derivation, is the adversary of God and is often defined as a fallen angel). Satanic cults have existed for centuries, partly originating in pre-Christian worship of demons and partly as a revolt against the Christian church (the rituals of Satanism are often travesties of Christian rituals, with, for example, a "black mass"). But ideas of Satanism go beyond the realm of Christendom: some mainstream Muslims, for example, accuse Iraq's Yazidi minority of Satanism. In 1966 Anton LaVey (1930–97), a former carnival performer, formed the Church of Satan in San Francisco, advocating indulgence of the senses among its few thousand followers.

Scandinavism Also known as Nordism or Scandinavianism, the term refers to the idea of a common cultural heritage shared by Norway, Sweden and Denmark. In the mid-19th century Scandinavism as a political movement envisioned a union between these three Scandinavian countries, paralleling the movements that led to the creation of modern Germany and Italy. This did not happen, but in many ways Scandinavism has succeeded in practical terms, with a passport union allowing passport-free travel between Norway, Sweden, Denmark, Finland and Iceland and with SAS – Scandinavian Airlines System, now called Scandinavian Airlines – formed after the second world war from the national airlines of Norway, Sweden and Denmark.

Schism From the Greek *skhisma*, meaning cleft, a split or division, especially in a religious community or political party. The so-called "East-West Schism" was the split in Christianity in 1054, finalised in the late 15th century, between the Eastern (Greek) and Western (Latin) churches (later known respectively as the Eastern Orthodox church and Roman Catholic church). The

"Great Schism", from 1378 to 1417, was the establishment of rival Roman Catholic papacies in Avignon and Rome. In Buddhism there have been many schisms, the first occurring within the Buddha's own lifetime. In Islam, the most obvious schism is between the Sunnis and the Shias (a split originally on political lines – *Shi'atu Ali* meant "party of Ali", the Prophet Muhammad's son-in-law – rather than on doctrinal ones).

Scholasticism A theological movement, beginning in the 11th century, that sought to reconcile the secular understanding of the world by Aristotle (384–322BC) and other classical philosophers with the dogmas of Christianity, notably its revelations. Leaders of the movement in its heyday in the 13th century included the French theologian Pierre Abélard (1079–1142), the English philosopher Roger Bacon (c1220–92) and, most notably, the Italian St Thomas Aquinas (c1225–74). By the 14th century scholasticism was in decline, with the Renaissance preferring the inductive reasoning of science (inferring particular instances from general laws) to the deductive reasoning of scholasticism (inferring the general from the particular). The word itself comes from the Latin *scholasticus*, meaning "belonging to the school", and has often carried the notion of a narrow-minded, adamant insistence on tradition.

Scientism The characteristic of being a scientist, or the belief (sometimes excessive, in a pejorative use of the word) in the power of science.

Sectarianism Adherence to the practices or doctrines of a sect, or faction, particularly a religious one (the Latin *secta* comes from the stem *sequi*, or follow). The word is almost always used in a pejorative sense, denoting discrimination or bigotry by one sect against another. Sectarianism is prevalent within many religions – for example, between Sunnis and Shias in Islam, or between Protestants and Roman Catholics in Christianity, or between Orthodox and Reform Jews – and has often been the cause of bloody conflict. Paradoxically, the recognition of sectarian differences is sometimes seen as a way of preventing conflict. Lebanon, for instance, allocates political power to some 18 different sects, from Maronites and Druzes to Greek Orthodox and Shias (a political compact that singularly failed to still the civil war of 1975–1990).

Secularism A way of thinking and action that rejects the involvement of religion – in other words, the separation of church and state. Public education in America, for example, is avowedly secular, and secularism – or *laïcité* – is a fundamental policy in France. The word is derived from the Latin *saeculum*, meaning generation or age, which was used in Christian Latin to mean the world, as opposed to the church. In the United States, secularism is often said to provide freedom for religion to flourish away from state control; in Europe, influenced by the Enlightenment's emphasis on science and rationality, secularism is generally thought of as freedom from religion. The term was first used in 1851 by an agnostic British writer, George Holyoake (1817–1906), who argued:

"Secularism is not an argument against Christianity, it is one independent of it."

Sensationalism The use of exciting imagery or language to arouse public interest. An example would be celebrity models posing naked as a protest against the wearing of fur. Sensationalism – often at the expense of accuracy – is a staple of tabloid journalism (the popular press), but is also frequent in political discourse. In philosophy, sensationalism is a synonym of phenomenalism (the notion that physical things exist only as phenomena perceived by the senses).

Sensualism The pursuit of sensual pleasure, especially in a sexual sense. In philosophy, sensualism – a term first used by Etienne de Condillac (1715–80), a French follower of the British philosopher John Locke (1632–1704) – is the doctrine that knowledge derives from the senses, free from any interpretation. Counted among the great philosophers of sensualism are Aristotle (384–322BC) in ancient Athens and St Thomas Aquinas (c1225–74) in 13th-century Italy. Aristotle's judgment was that "there is nothing in the mind which has not been before in the senses" (*nihil est in intellectu nisi quod antea fuerit in sensu*), as the Germany philosopher Arthur Schopenhauer (1788–1860) translated Aristotle into Latin in the 19th century.

Separatism The advocacy of separation of a minority from a larger body, usually on the basis of religion or ethnicity. Examples have existed throughout history. In the 16th and 17th century, for example, nonconformist Christians in Britain separated themselves from the Anglican church, setting up independent churches, some of which became the Congregationalist church (see **Congregationalism**). More recent examples are Tamil demands for a separate state in Sinhalese-dominated Sri Lanka; Kurdish demands for a separate state in the nexus of Iraq, Turkey and Iran; and the armed struggle for a separate Muslim state in the southern islands of the Catholic-dominated Philippines.

Serialism A technique in musical composition in which a fixed series of notes – normally the 12 notes of the chromatic scale – produces the melody or harmony. The first fully serial movements were those of the Austrian-born American composer Arnold Schoenberg (1874–1951) in 1923. Serialism is often known as 12-tone, but the 12-tone method is just one of several kinds of serialism. Basic to the technique is a quasi-mathematical method of choosing which notes to use and when. The result often seems random to the listener, and is certainly far removed from the "traditional" music of composers such as Johann Sebastian Bach (1685–1750) and Wolfgang Amadeus Mozart (1756–91). Exponents of serialism include Igor Stravinsky (1882–1971), Karl-Heinz Stockhausen (1928–2007), Dmitri Shostakovich (1906–75) and Pierre Boulez – and also jazz composers such as Bill Evans (1929–80).

Sexism Discrimination, usually against women, on the basis of a person's sex and rooted in the belief that one sex is superior to the other. The term originated in the mid-20th century as part of the vocabulary of the feminist movement. Sexism has doubtless existed for millennia in most societies – and is certainly a feature of modern life, too. For example, women did not get the vote in America until 1920, in Britain 1928, in France 1944 and in Switzerland 1971. In the 21st century, despite equal-opportunity legislation in many countries, a wage gap continues to exist between men and women. Even in the United States, a bastion of feminism, a woman on average earns only 75% of a man's wage.

Shamanism The practice and beliefs of shamans, "medicine men" in northern Asia and North America, with access to both good and evil spirits and acting as intermediaries between the human and spirit worlds. A shaman will typically enter a trance while healing a disease or divining the future.

Shiism One of the two main branches of Islam (the other, much larger, being Sunni). Shiism is the majority denomination in Iran and, to a lesser extent, in Iraq. The word originates in the Arabic term *Shi'atu Ali*, meaning the party or faction of Ali ibn Abi Talib (c600–661), the cousin and son-in-law of the Prophet Muhammad. Ali was the fourth caliph (or successor, from 656 to 661) in Islam after the death of Muhammad, but Ali's followers held that he should have been the first. What was originally a political split with the Sunnis later became a doctrinal one (not least as the Shias in Iran were influenced by pre-existing Zoroastrianism), with a distinct Shia, metaphysically inclined, theology emerging in the second century after Muhammad's death. Shiism holds that the Muslim *ummah*, or community, should be led by an imam (with an infallibility similar to that of the pope in Christendom), descended from Muhammad's family. Ali was therefore the first imam. Shias variously believe that the imam became hidden, either after the 12th imam in the 9th century (hence the "Twelvers", or mainstream Shias), the seventh (hence the "Seveners", who are a faction of the Ismailis, who in turn are led by the Aga Khan and are prominent in India and East Africa) or the fifth (hence the "Fivers" or Zaydis, concentrated in Yemen). Other Shia offshoots, minorities in their countries, are the Druzes of Lebanon and the Alawis of Syria. The Twelvers believe that the 12th imam, Muhammad ibn al-Hassan, will return as the Mahdi (the Guided One) to save mankind.

Shintoism The main religion of Japan, with around 119m adherents. It originated in around 500BC as an amalgam of animism and shamanism, but became codified in the 8th century AD, taking its name from the Chinese *shin tao*, or "Way of the Gods", and ascribing divinity to the ruling imperial family (the separation of religion from politics took place only after Japan's defeat in the second world war). Shintoism, which is heavily influenced by Confucianism, has "four affirmations": tradition and the family; the sacredness of nature; cleanliness; and the honouring of ancestral spirits and of the supernatural forces and deities known as Kami.

Sikhism A monotheistic religion founded in Punjab in the 15th century by Guru Nanak Dev (1469–1539), the first of ten Sikh gurus (teachers), and practised by more than 20m believers in India and the Indian diaspora. According to the beliefs set out in a text – the Guru Granth Sahib, or "revered book" – decreed by the tenth and last guru, Gobind Singh (1666–1708), in the early 18th century, God is universal and without form or gender; everyone is equal before God and has direct access to God; and humans exist in a cycle of birth, life and rebirth, with the quality of their lives determined by the law of karma – the balance of good and evil in their previous lives. The five vices to be fought against are lust, greed, materialism, anger and pride. Baptised Sikhs, known as the *Khalsa* (from the Arabic for pure), identify themselves with the five Ks: *Kesh*, or uncut hair; *Kara*, a metal bracelet; *Kanga*, a wooden comb; *Kacha*, a cotton undergarment; and *Kirpan*, a dagger.

Social Darwinism The theory that people are subject to the same Darwinian laws of natural selection as plants and animals. The theory was advanced most notably by Herbert Spencer (1820–1903), a British sociologist and philosopher, and by Charles Darwin's cousin, Francis Galton (1822–1911), and has been variously used to justify colonialism, racism and eugenics (Adolf Hitler was an obvious convert to the theory). The impact of eugenics in America was such that from 1910 to 1930 some 24 states passed sterilisation laws, and Congress restricted immigration from certain areas deemed to be unfit. The influence of social Darwinism was not, however, entirely negative: philanthropists such as the Scottish-American Andrew Carnegie (1835–1919) opposed uniform handouts to the poor but gave handsomely to the "deserving poor". Indeed, in Britain, the concept of the deserving poor was fundamental to the social reforms carried out by the Liberal Party in the early 20th century.

Socialism A political and economic theory that holds that the means of production and distribution in an economy should be owned or regulated by the community as a whole or by a central government. In Marxist theory, socialism is the transitional stage between capitalism and communism. In practice, socialism is a broad-brush term embracing everything from Marxism to the social democracy found in much of Europe. Common to all systems, however, is a belief in the need for collective intervention – as in the welfare state – in economic affairs and a desire to lessen social inequality. Socialism developed in the late 18th and early 19th centuries as a reaction against the negative effects of industrialisation. Prominent early advocates were the British social reformer Robert Owen (1771–1858), a founder of the co-operative movement, and Henri de Saint-Simon (1760–1825), a French utopian thinker who is credited with being the first to use the term *socialisme*. The popularity of socialism has fluctuated over the decades. During the cold war the communist world considered itself socialist, and after the second world war several west European countries periodically elected social-democratic governments, mixing elements of government intervention with capitalism. By contrast, America,

despite centrally planned measures such as Medicare and
Social Security, has always considered socialism a threat
to its way of life, with the word almost invariably used
pejoratively.

Solecism A mistake in grammar, or – by extension – a breach
of etiquette. The word comes from the Greek *soloikos*,
which means speaking incorrectly, apparently a
characteristic of the inhabitants of Soloi, an ancient
Athenian colony in Cilicia. An example of a solecism is
the phrase "between you and I", rather than the correct
"between you and me".

Solipsism The view that the self is all that can be proven to
exist. The derivation is from the Latin *solus*, meaning
alone, and *ipse*, meaning self. As Francis Herbert Bradley
(1846-1924), a British philosopher, put it in 1897: "I cannot
transcend experience, and experience is my experience.
From this it follows that nothing beyond myself exists; for
what is experience is its (the self's) states."

Sophism A clever but specious argument (from the Greek
sophisma, meaning clever device, itself derived from
sophizesthai, to become wise). In ancient Greece, the
sophists were professional teachers of rhetoric and
reasoning and were important in the development of law.
Over time, however, sophism has taken on a disparaging
sense, as in sophistry: the use of subtle, clever yet
fallacious arguments.

Spiritualism The notion that the spirits of the dead communicate with the living, especially through the agency of mediums – people (usually women) supposedly able to be in contact with the spirits. Spiritualism, in many ways similar to shamanism, has coexisted with several religions, with many spiritualists in America and Europe counting themselves as Christians. In Judaism, however, it is forbidden, with God telling Moses in Leviticus: "I will set my face against the person who turns to mediums and spiritists to prostitute himself by following them, and I will cut him off from his people."

Spoonerism The accidental transposition of initial sounds in two or more words, often to humorous effect – as in "our queer old dean", instead of "our dear old queen", or "wave the sails" instead of "save the whales". The term is derived from the Reverend William Archibald Spooner (1844–1930), a British scholar, whose speech was apparently prone to such errors (one alleged example was "The Lord is a shoving leopard").

Stalinism The ideology and practices of Joseph Stalin (1879–1953), the ruthless general secretary of the Communist Party of the Soviet Union from 1922 to 1953. Apart from the brutal repression of any perceived dissent, Stalinism was characterised by a command economy, with successive five-year plans (the first included the collectivisation of agriculture); rapid industrialisation; and the control of eastern Europe (the Eastern Bloc) after the second world war behind what Churchill called "the Iron

Curtain". The term was originally coined in a positive sense by an aide of Stalin, Lazar Kaganovich (Stalin himself rejected the term). Such was the cruelty of Stalin's rule, however, that the word is invariably used in a pejorative sense, reflecting the millions executed, imprisoned or starved during that time. Indeed, Stalin's successor, Nikita Khrushchev (1894–1971), criticised Stalin's personality cult and began a programme of modest liberalisation. Ironically, in the 21st century in newly democratic Russia, which has abandoned communism for capitalism, there have been government-inspired moves to rehabilitate Stalin's image.

Statism A political system in which the central government has a major, even dominant, role in economic and social planning. Statism has been connected with both fascism – as in Nazi Germany – and communism, as in the Soviet Union. In reality, however, most countries have exercised a degree of statism, depending on the size of the public sector (through, for example, state-owned industries, public housing or state-run services).

Stoicism An uncomplaining indifference to hardship or pain. More particularly, Stoicism refers to the philosophy taught in Athens by Zeno of Citium (335–263BC). The Stoics took their name from the *Stoa Poikile* (the "painted porch" of a colonnade where Zeno taught) and believed that virtue, based on reason, involves living in harmony with fate and what fate decrees. It follows that man should free himself from passion and emotion. Stoicism flourished as a philosophy (albeit not as a common way of life) for

centuries in the Greco-Roman world. As Epictetus
(c55–135AD), a Greek Stoic who lived in Rome (initially as
a slave), put it: "Freedom is secured not by the fulfilling of
one's desires, but by the removal of desire."

Structuralism A method of interpreting phenomena –
particularly in anthropology, linguistics, literature and
psychology – by contrasting in a binary opposition the
elements of their structure. Structuralism developed
principally in 20th-century France, drawing on the
theories of the Swiss linguist Ferdinand de Saussure
(1857–1913), who held that language is a system of signs,
and the Belgian-born French anthropologist Claude
Lévi-Strauss (1908–2009), who believed that cultures, too,
are systems of signs. Basic to structuralism is the notion
of opposites, as in male/female, cooked/raw and public/
private. In a broader sense, structuralism as an
intellectual movement argues that the phenomena of
existence are not intelligible except through
understanding their interrelationship.

Sufism An esoteric, ascetic and mystical form of Islam. Sufis
(the word comes from the Arabic *suf*, or wool –
apparently a reference to the Sufis' clothing – although
rival explanations point to *safa*, the Arabic word for
purity, or to the Greek *sophia*, meaning wisdom) are
found in both Sunni and Shia Islam. As the great Arab
historian Ibn Khaldun (1332–1406) put it, Sufism is
dedication to "Allah most High, disregard for the finery
and ornament of the world, abstinence from the pleasure,
wealth, and prestige sought by most men, and retiring

from others to worship alone". Sufism, with its devotion to the remembrance of Allah (*dhikr Allah*) through meditation and dance or the repetition of the names of Allah, began as a reaction against the lax excess of the Umayyad caliphate (661-750AD), but its high point was in the 13th century, by which time, as it spread through the Muslim world, it had absorbed influences from other religions such as Buddhism and Zoroastrianism. There are several Sufi orders or *turuq*, with the Mevlevi or Mawlawi order, founded in Konya, Turkey, in the 13th century as followers of the Persian poet Rumi, being known as the "whirling Dervishes" after their practice of whirling in a trance as a form of *dhikr*.

Surrealism A revolutionary movement in art and literature, formally identified in a 1924 manifesto by the French poet and writer André Breton (1896-1966). Surrealism drew much of its inspiration from the Dada school of art (see Dadaism) and from the teachings of Sigmund Freud (1856-1939). The aim was to release the potential of the unconscious mind by the seemingly irrational juxtaposition of images, for example in the hallucinogenic painting by the Spanish artist Salvador Dali (1904-89) of a beach festooned with distorted watches or the painting by the Belgian artist René Magritte (1898-1967) of a bowler-hatted businessman with an apple in front of his face. Other prominent surrealists included the German artist Max Ernst (1891-1976), the Spanish artist Joan Miró (1893-1983) and, in the cinema, the Spanish director Luis Buñuel (1900-83).

Syllogism A form of deductive reasoning (derived from the
Greek *sun*, meaning with, and *logizesthai*, to reason) in
which the conclusion is drawn from two propositions
that share a term with the conclusion while also sharing
a term not included in the conclusion. The result can be
true, but often is false. As an example of the former: all
cats are animals and all animals have four limbs –
therefore all cats have four limbs. As an example of the
latter: all cats have four legs; this horse has four legs
– therefore this horse is a cat.

Symbolism The use of symbols to represent ideas – for
example, the cross for Christianity and the crescent for
Islam. As a cultural phenomenon, symbolism was a
movement in the arts and poetry that used symbolic
imagery to express emotions. It originated in France and
Belgium in the late 19th century, with the Greek-born
Jean Moréas (1856–1910) publishing *The Symbolist
Manifesto* in *Le Figaro* newspaper in 1886. The poets
Stéphane Mallarmé (1842–98), Paul Verlaine (1844–96) and
Arthur Rimbaud (1854–91) can all be counted as
symbolists, along with the painters Gustave Moreau
(1826–98), Odilon Redon (1840–1916) and Pierre Puvis de
Chavannes (1824–98).

Syndicalism A system to replace capitalism and the role of the
state by transferring the ownership and control of the
means of production to trade unions, which would then
manage the economy through co-operatives. The word
comes from the French *syndicalisme*, or trade unionism,
with the concept originating in the ideas of the French

anarchist Pierre-Joseph Proudhon (1809–65), famous for declaring that "property is theft", and a compatriot, the social philosopher Georges Sorel (1847–1922). Syndicalism flourished in France and elsewhere in Europe in the early 20th century but by the end of the first world war had ceased to be important.

t

Tantrism A religious philosophy, found in much of Asia, that involves adherence to the teachings of the tantras – Hindu and Buddhist mystical texts dating from the 6th to the 13th centuries – and practices such as meditation and yoga. The term comes from the Sanskrit *tan*, meaning loom or weave, denoting in this sense continuity. Basic to tantrism is the idea of channelling universal energy to seek the liberation of the self.

Taoism A Chinese philosophy, derived from the teachings of Lao-tzu (also transliterated as Laozi and literally meaning old man), a 6th-century BC contemporary of Confucius (551–479BC), which emphasises humility and piety. *Tao* (sometimes transliterated as *Dao*) roughly means "the way", and is thought of as a force running through life and embodying the harmony of opposites, as in male and female or light and dark (the yin-yang symbol, reflecting the balance of opposites, belongs to Taoism). In the 5th century AD Taoism, which had adopted many of the features of **Buddhism**, became a state-recognised religion in China with its own system of monasteries (state support ended in 1911 with the collapse of the Ching dynasty). Basic to Taoism is the concept of *wu-wei*, "action without action" – or letting nature take its course. A river, for example, may simply be the flow of water, but it can move earth and carve stone, and so should not be checked by a dam. As Lao-tzu advised: "Be still like a mountain and flow like a great river."

Taylorism The principles of scientific management, developed in the 1880s–90s by Frederick Winslow Taylor (1856–1915), an American engineer, by analysing the flow of work in a factory. Taylor's book, *The Principles of Scientific Management*, was published in 1911 and, like Fordism, helped promote the quest for industrial efficiency. Taylorism breaks down manufacturing into the smallest and simplest units so that unskilled workers can concentrate on simple, repetitive tasks, supervised by decision-making managers. The result was to be increased productivity (albeit at the expense of bored workers).

An entirely different Taylorism, also known as New Haven theology, is a form of Calvinism named after a 19th-century American theologian, Nathaniel William Taylor (1786–1858), who taught that man has free will, which makes possible a distinction between depravity (the tendency to commit sins) and sin (a voluntary choice to commit evil). Unlike traditional Calvinism, Taylorism does not hold that sin and depravity are innate; rather they are the consequence of choice. "There is no such thing," Taylor wrote, "as sinning without acting."

Terrorism The use or threat of violence for political purposes, in other words the use of terror to achieve a goal. Terrorism is doubtless as old as mankind, but there is no universally agreed definition of what constitutes terror. The French Revolution was followed, by government decree in 1793–94, by what Robespierre (1758–94), its prime advocate, called the "Reign of Terror", arguing that "terror is nothing other than justice, prompt, severe, inflexible". In normal usage, however, terrorism is a pejorative term, implying the infliction of terror on innocent non-combatants. American federal regulations state that terrorism is "the unlawful use of force and violence against persons or property to intimidate or coerce a government, the civilian population, or any segment thereof, in furtherance of political or social objectives". The problem, as governments – especially during the 20th-century struggles of decolonisation – have frequently discovered, is that one person's terrorist is another's freedom fighter. America considered Afghan *mujahideen* to be freedom fighters in their battles with the Soviet Union in the late 20th century, but called the same *mujahideen* terrorists when they turned against American and NATO troops in the early 21st century.

One more recent concept is that of state-sponsored terrorism: the employment by governments of non-state agents to carry out acts of terror (America, for example, has frequently accused Syria and Iran of sponsoring actions by Hizbullah, which it considers a terrorist organisation, against Israel). State terrorism is a controversial term referring to the use of terror by governments – a definition that implies war crimes and could (according to some scholars) cover actions such as the dropping of atomic bombs by America on Hiroshima and Nagasaki in the second world war or the launching by Germany during the second world war of V-2 rockets against London.

Another addition to the vocabulary of terrorism is the term "cyber-terrorism", meaning attempts, by state and non-state actors, to cause alarm by damaging computer networks, especially in the financial and government sectors.

Thatcherism The political ideology and style of Margaret Thatcher, Conservative prime minister in the UK from 1979 to 1990. Mrs (later Baroness) Thatcher espoused free-market economics and a diminished role for the state. As such she presided over the privatisation of many of Britain's state-owned assets (for example, the British Steel Corporation, British Airways and the telephone network – which had belonged to the post office but was branded British Telecom in 1980 as a prelude to privatisation). Thatcherism was in many ways a parallel to Reaganism in America, with both Reagan and Thatcher influenced by Milton Friedman (1912–2006) and other monetarist economists (see monetarism). Thatcherism, however, because its influence continued under John Major, prime minister from 1990 until 1997, lasted considerably longer than Reagan's eight years in office. Nigel Lawson, Mrs Thatcher's chancellor of the exchequer from 1983 to 1989, defined Thatcherism as "free markets, financial discipline, firm control over public expenditure, tax cuts, nationalism, 'Victorian values' (of the Samuel

Smiles self-help variety), privatisation and a dash of populism". Thatcherism also involved a successful determination to limit the power of British trade unions, notably in defeating a 1984–85 strike by Britain's coal miners (who, in a strike in the 1970s, had humiliated a previous Conservative prime minister, Edward Heath). In foreign policy, Thatcherism was marked by a robust **nationalism**, for example in defeating Argentina's invasion of the Falkland Islands and in achieving a substantial rebate from Britain's contribution to the budget of the European Union – a structure for which Mrs Thatcher showed considerable mistrust. "We have not successfully rolled back the frontiers of the state in Britain," she argued in 1988, "only to see them reimposed at a European level, with a European superstate exercising a new dominance from Brussels."

Theism The belief in a god or gods, especially in one god as creator of the universe. Whereas **deism** believes that such a god does not intervene in the doings of mankind, theism holds that the creator of the universe maintains a personal and active relationship with his creatures. The word (from the Greek *theos*, or god) was first used by Ralph Cudworth (1617–88), a British philosopher and theologian, in contrast to the theory of deism emerging from the advance during the Enlightenment of scientific thought and rationality.

Totalitarianism A dictatorial and centralised system of government that demands subservience by citizens to the state, which has no limits to its authority. Totalitarian governments have existed for millennia (for example, China's Qin dynasty in the 3rd century BC), but the term probably originates with Benito Mussolini (1883–1945), the fascist leader of Italy, in the 1920s. Communist regimes, from the former Soviet Union to modern China, are invariably defined as totalitarian (see communism).

Totemism The idea, common in history to most parts of the world and held in particular by native Americans, that a natural object or animal has a spiritual importance and so should be used as a spiritual symbol – or totem. The word "totem", first used in the mid-18th century, is derived from the Ojibwa (a native American tribe) word *ototeman*, used to signify a blood relationship. Basic to totemism is an animistic view of existence (see animism), often with shamans to interpret the relationship between humans and the spirit world (see shamanism). Contact with a totem is almost always carefully regulated, involving various taboos or, indeed, avoidance. The totem poles found in North America are not actually totems but rather symbols of heraldry, depicting, for example, the history of the clan or tribe.

Transcendentalism A philosophical movement founded in New England in the 19th century that emphasised an ideal spiritual state that "transcends" physical reality and can be attained only by an individual's intuition, rather than by the practices of established religions: man is innately good and reaches the most profound truth through insight rather than by experience or logic. The movement began in 1836 with an essay by the American writer Ralph Waldo Emerson (1803–82), followed in the same year by the establishment of the Transcendental Club in Cambridge, Massachusetts. Prominent transcendentalists included the poet Walt Whitman (1819–92) and Henry David Thoreau (1817–62), whose book *Walden*, praising a simple life in idyllically natural surroundings, paid tribute to the influence on the movement of Vedic thought. The transcendentalists were inspired by romanticism, Platonism and the work of the German philosopher Immanuel Kant (1724–1804), whose transcendental philosophy emphasised what lies beyond the limits of experience. The transcendentalist movement was therefore a reaction against rationalism, and in particular against the predominant thinking of the time at Harvard University.

Transvestism (or transvesticism) The practice of dressing in the clothes of the opposite sex – most commonly involving a man deriving pleasure from dressing as a woman. The term, literally cross-dressing, from its Latin roots, originated in the early 20th-century writings of Magnus Hirschfeld (1868–1935), a homosexual German physician and early campaigner for gay rights, but clearly transvestism has existed for centuries in many cultures. Transvestism does not always have a sexual connotation: in many Shakespearean plays women dress as men in order to carry out actions difficult for women – as in Portia appearing in court to plead the case of the merchant in *The Merchant of Venice*. Male actors dressed as women remain a staple of British pantomime.

Triumphalism An excessive joy in victory, especially in a political context. More generally, the term implies the belief that a particular set of values, or a particular religion or culture, is superior to others. As such, triumphalism is often linked to the foreign policy of imperial powers.

Tropism A biological phenomenon, usually of plants, in which an organism turns or grows in a particular direction in response to an external stimulus (as sunflowers to the sun). The word, originating in the late 19th century and derived from the Greek *tropos*, or turning, has many prefixes: geotropism, for example, involves a plant growing downwards in response to gravity; phototropism involves a reaction to light; and haptotropism happens when a plant reacts to touch, as when a climbing vine wraps around a support.

Trotskyism The Marxist doctrine of Leon Trotsky (1879–1940), a leader of the 1917 Russian revolution (he was banished from the Soviet Union in 1929 and later sought exile in Mexico, where he was assassinated by a blow from an ice-axe in 1940). Fundamental to Trotskyism is the theory of permanent revolution as the means to establish socialism worldwide, rather than in an individual country (as Stalinism argued for Russia). The term nowadays is often used to describe almost any radical form of socialism, often implying an element of anarchism too.

u

Ultramontanism The doctrine that the pope has supreme authority – superior, for example, to that of local authorities and bishops – in the Roman Catholic church in matters of faith and discipline. The word, derived from the Latin *ultra*, meaning beyond, and *mons*, meaning mountain, was originally used in the Middle Ages to describe a non-Italian pope as being from "beyond the mountains" – that is the Alps separating the Italian peninsula from the north. In France, after the 16th-century Protestant Reformation, the geography of the word was reversed to describe the papal authority resident in Italy, the implication being that followers of the doctrine were less patriotic than the Gallican – that is, French – stream of the Catholic church in France, which asserted that authority in the church should be shared with the monarch (see **Gallicanism**).

Uniformitarianism The theory that the universe is subject to unchanging laws, independent of time, so that "the present is the key to the past". The implication in geology, as argued in the late 18th century by the Scottish geologist

James Hutton (1726–97), was that changes in the Earth's crust over the millennia resulted from the action of continuous and uniform processes. In Hutton's view, the Earth had "no vestige of a beginning, no prospect of an end". The term was coined by William Whewell (1794–1866), an English scientist, who also coined the term catastrophism for the counter-theory that the Earth was shaped by a series of sudden and violent events (such as the Biblical flood).

Unilateralism The process of acting without the collaboration of others. The term is usually employed in a political context, as in the argument for unilateral nuclear disarmament. In foreign policy, unilateralism is frequently linked with isolationism (America's first president, George Washington, famously said in his farewell address in 1796: "'Tis our true policy to steer clear of permanent Alliances, with any portion of the foreign world"), but there is clearly no necessary connection. One more recent example of American unilateralism was President George W. Bush's statement in 2002 that "our security will require all Americans to be forward-looking and resolute, to be ready for pre-emptive action when necessary to defend our liberty and to defend our lives" – a clear pledge that America was willing to act alone if it felt threatened.

Unionism The practice of forming a union – for example, a trade union. The term also applies to the opposition to the secession of the South during the American civil war and, in modern times, to the advocacy in Northern

Ireland of continued union with Britain (hence, the United Kingdom of Great Britain and Ireland, formed by the 1800 Act of Union, later to become the United Kingdom of Great Britain and Northern Ireland following the independence from British rule of 26 southern Irish counties in 1922).

Unitarianism The assertion of the unity of God and therefore the rejection of the conventional Christian doctrine of the Trinity (of God as the Father, the Son and the Holy Ghost). Unitarianism, which grew out of the 16th-century Protestant Reformation, originating in Poland and Transylvania, has no creed; but Unitarians, who now number about 800,000 worldwide, over a quarter of them in America, emphasise the oneness of god and the essential unity of creation. Unitarian universalism happily embraces Christians, Jews, Buddhists, humanists and spiritualists.

Universalism A Christian theology that holds that all mankind will eventually be saved. As a result there is a heaven but no hell. The concept of universalism was present in the earliest days of Christianity but was controversial, with opposing doctrines preaching eternal damnation for lost souls. Wider acceptance came in 17th-century Europe. More generally, the term means the promotion of concern for others regardless of nationality or other individual allegiance. In this sense, universalism is a characteristic of many religions, with Islam, for example, preaching universal brotherhood.

Utilitarianism The doctrine that virtue is based on utility, and so the correct aim of an action should be to promote the greatest happiness for the greatest number. Utilitarianism goes back to Epicureanism and hedonism, but was defined in its modern form by the British philosopher and social reformer Jeremy Bentham (1748–1832), who wrote: "Nature has placed mankind under the governance of two sovereign masters, pain and pleasure. It is for them alone to point out what we ought to do, as well as to determine what we shall do." The most prominent exponent of the doctrine, however, was the British philosopher John Stuart Mill (1806–73), who wrote in *Utilitarianism*, published in 1863: "The creed which accepts as the foundation of morals, utility or the greatest happiness principle, holds that actions are right in proportion as they tend to promote happiness, wrong as they tend to produce the reverse of happiness. By happiness is intended pleasure and the absence of pain; by unhappiness, pain and the privation of pleasure." Whereas Bentham treated all forms of happiness as equal, Mill thought happiness to be superior to contentment, and intellectual satisfaction superior to physical satisfaction, arguing that it is "better to be a human being dissatisfied than a pig satisfied; better to be Socrates dissatisfied than a fool satisfied. And if the fool, or the pig, are of a different opinion, it is because they only know their own side of the question".

Utopianism The feeling that everything is, or could be, perfect. The term comes from the title of a 1516 book, inspired by Plato's *Republic*, by Sir Thomas More (beheaded in 1535 by Henry VIII). *Utopia* describes the imaginary Atlantic island of Utopia, where the social, political and legal systems were perfect – but the very word is a play on words: the derivation from the Greek can be either from *eu*, meaning good, and *topos*, meaning place, or from *ou*, meaning not, and *topos*. Utopian socialism, a term used by Marx and Engels to refer to all visionary socialist ideas, is the notion that if capital gave ownership of the means of production to the workers or the state, unemployment and poverty would be abolished. Perhaps not surprisingly, utopian is normally used as a synonym for fanciful or unrealistic.

V

Valetudinarianism Being excessively worried about being ill or being in poor health – not quite the same as hypochondria, since the ill health may be genuine. The term, originating in the early 18th century, is derived from the Latin *valetudinarius*, meaning "in ill health", which comes in turn from *valetudo*, "state of health or sickness", from *valere*, "to be well".

Vandalism The act or process of intentionally damaging public or private property, from daubing walls with graffiti to breaking windows. The term, which often denotes minor rather than serious damage or destruction, is a reference to the Vandals, a Germanic people who ravaged much of western Europe and north Africa in the 4th and 5th centuries, sacking Rome itself in 455 in what was seen by historians and writers in the 17th century as an orgy of senseless destruction. The French word *vandalisme* was probably coined in 1794 by a French bishop, Henri Grégoire (1750–1831), to describe the destruction of works of art following the French Revolution.

Veganism A lifestyle that excludes all animal products, be they meat and honey in the diet or leather in shoes. Vegans are thus different from vegetarians, who will, for example, consume eggs and milk or wear leather or fur. The word "vegan" was coined in 1944 by Donald Watson, the British founder of the Vegan Society (he died in 2005 at the age of 95), from the first three and last two letters of "vegetarian" as "the beginning and the end of vegetarian". Underlying veganism is an ethical stance that animals have a right not to be exploited.

Vegetarianism The practice – for moral, religious or health reasons – of excluding meat, and usually fish, too, from the diet. The Vegetarian Society, founded in Britain in 1847, claims to have invented the term from the Latin *vegetus*, meaning lively (the result, apparently, of the diet), as a successor to the previous term "Pythagorean": Pythagoras (c570–495BC), the Greek philosopher, was a vegetarian. However, several dictionaries conclude that the word was formed from "vegetable" and the suffix "-arian" and existed earlier; for example, Fanny Kemble (1809–83), writing in her *Journal of a Residence on a Georgian Plantation in 1838–39*, said: "If I had had to be my own cook, I should inevitably become a vegetarian." Followers of both Hinduism and Jainism practise vegetarianism, as do many Buddhists. In the West, vegetarianism has become increasingly popular since the latter part of the 20th century, particularly because of the reported health benefits of a meat-free diet.

Vorticism A short-lived movement in British art, lasting from 1913 for about three years (only one exhibition, in 1915, was ever held). Vorticism had its roots in **cubism** and **futurism**, though its leading practitioner, Percy Wyndham Lewis (1882–1957), saw it as an alternative to those schools of art. The term was coined in 1913 by the American expatriate poet Ezra Pound (1885–1972). In a Vorticist painting the lines and shapes draw the viewer's eye to the centre of the canvas.

Voyeurism The practice of gaining sexual pleasure by watching – usually unseen – others who are naked or engaged in sexual activity. A voyeur (a French noun from the verb *voir*, meaning to see) is colloquially known as a "peeping Tom".

Vulgarism A crude or rude expression, particularly one connected with sex or bodily functions. The derivation is from the Latin *vulgus*, meaning common people or rabble. Vulgarisms have existed for millennia and vary with generations and cultures. In Britain, for example, the word "bloody" remains impolite and so offensive to many ears, but in Australia it is a commonplace, even in Parliament.

W

Wahhabism A severely austere and orthodox form of Sunni Islam and the dominant religious force in Saudi Arabia and Qatar. The term comes from the name of the sect's founder, Muhammad ibn Abd al-Wahhab (1703-92), an Islamic scholar born in the Najd region of the Arabian peninsula. Ibn Abd al-Wahhab's emphasis on returning to the purity of Islam's origins meant that he opposed innovation and the idea of intercession between a believer and Allah – a stance that puts Wahhabism at odds with Sufism and Shiism. Wahhabism's influence stems from its embrace by Muhammad ibn Saud (died 1765) in 1744. The subsequent dominance of the Saud family, culminating in the establishment of the Kingdom of Saudi Arabia in 1932, ensured the continuing power of Wahhabism and its cultural features, such as the segregation of the sexes and a ban on cinemas.

Whiggism The doctrine of the Whigs, a British political faction – particularly powerful in the 18th century – that later became the Liberal Party. The word "Whig", probably derived from the Scottish *whiggamore* or cattle driver, was first used by Scottish Presbyterians around 1679 as a term of abuse against English opponents of the succession to the throne of the Roman Catholic convert, the Duke of York (who became James II, ruling from 1685 to 1688). In the bloodless Glorious Revolution of 1688–89 the Whigs succeeded in forcing the abdication of James II and bringing about the restoration of a Protestant monarchy in the shape of William of Orange (invited to come from the Netherlands) and his wife Mary (who was the daughter of the deposed James), who ruled from 1689 to 1702 (Mary died in 1694). The Whigs, whose political rivals were the Tories, were in government for most of the 18th century, in opposition for most of the period that followed the 1789 French Revolution, and in government again after the reform act of 1832, which granted seats in Parliament to the cities spawned by the industrial revolution and eliminated many of the rural "rotten boroughs". It was in the aftermath of the reform act that a middle-class stream of Whigs formed the Liberal Party in opposition to aristocratic Whigs resistant to further electoral reforms.

In America, the Whig Party existed from 1834 to 1854, taking its name from the British Whigs on the ground that the British Whigs opposed royal prerogatives and the American Whigs were opposed to what they viewed as the executive tyranny of "King Andrew" Jackson, America's president from 1829 to 1837. The American Whigs, who later became the Republican Party, never developed a defined party programme but still managed to elect as president in 1840 William Henry Harrison, who then died after just one month in office. They had to wait until 1849 before getting another Whig, Zachary Taylor, elected president (he died in 1850), but by then the Whigs were dividing into "Conscience" Whigs, opposed to slavery, and "Cotton" Whigs, supporting slavery. The result was that in 1854 the Whig Party collapsed, with northern Whigs joining the newly formed Republican Party.

White nationalism A political ideology advocating a racial definition of national identity and believing in the supremacy of cultures originating in white European stock. According to Samuel Todd Francis (1947–2005), an American newspaper columnist opposed to immigration and multiculturalism, white nationalism is "a movement that rejects equality as an ideal and insists on an enduring core of human nature transmitted by heredity". "White Power" became a slogan in the latter half of the 20th century of the American Nazi Party, in opposition to the "Black Power" slogan of groups such as the Black Panthers. Though not using the actual term, white nationalism underlay the apartheid policy of South Africa from 1948 until the early 1990s; it was also implicit in the "White Australia" immigration policy of Australia from 1901 to 1973.

Witticism A clever and often amusing remark, frequently by playing on words. The term was coined in 1677 by the British poet and dramatist John Dryden (1631–1700) from the adjective "witty" (Middle English for clever or ingenious). A great producer of witticisms was the Irish playwright Oscar Wilde (1854–1900), with examples such as "I have nothing to declare but my genius" and "I am not young enough to know everything".

Z

Zeism A skin condition, such as pellagra, associated with an excessive proportion in the diet of maize (which is low in zinc and niacin).

Zionism A movement for the establishment in Palestine – and now the protection – of a national homeland for Jews. The word originates with Mount Zion, a mountain near Jerusalem, which in the era of King David in the 10th century BC became a term for the whole Land of Israel. Zionism was founded as a political organisation by Theodor Herzl (1860–1904), a Hungarian Jew, who had first encountered anti-Semitism while studying in Vienna and had later experienced the anti-Semitism of France during the "Dreyfus affair" of 1894. Herzl, who published *Der Judenstaat* (The Jewish State) in 1896, concluded that anti-Semitism was a fundamental characteristic of human society that would not be solved by assimilation. Acceptance of Jews would only happen with their establishment as a nation with a home of their own. Initially, wealthy Jews were not impressed by this idea, but Herzl nonetheless organised the first Zionist Congress in Basel, Switzerland, in 1897, "to establish a home for the Jewish people in Palestine secured under public law" (Herzl envisaged this as a socialist utopia). As a temporary measure Herzl was attracted by a British offer of an autonomous Jewish region in Uganda, but the Seventh Zionist Congress rejected the idea in 1905.

A great boost to Zionism came when Chaim Weizmann (1874–1952), a Russian Jew, persuaded Britain, perhaps fearing that American Jews would convince America to side with Germany in the first world war, to issue the Balfour Declaration of 1917, endorsing the creation of a Jewish homeland in Palestine, "it being clearly understood that nothing shall be done which may prejudice the civil and religious rights of existing non-Jewish communities in Palestine". This project was then confirmed by the League of Nations in 1922. The fulfilment of Zionism, as Europe and America recognised the horrors of the Nazi Holocaust, came first in 1947 with the UN partition plan for Palestine and then with the establishment of the state of Israel in May 1948.

The World Zionist Organisation today encourages Jewish immigration to Israel, but Zionism remains controversial because of the continuing plight of the Palestinians, especially in areas outside Israel but controlled by Israel. In 1975, despite uproar in the West, the UN passed Resolution 3379, declaring "Zionism is a form of racism and racial discrimination" (the Resolution was revoked – the only instance in UN history – in 1991).

Zoomorphism The representation – for example in pottery – of animal forms, especially of gods in the form of

animals. The word is derived from the Greek *zoon*,
meaning animal, and *morphe*, meaning form.

Zoroastrianism A monotheistic religion, also known as
Mazdaism, founded in Persia (now Iran) by the prophet
Zoroaster (also spelled Zarathustra), who lived from
around 628 to 551 BC. Zoroaster taught that the supreme
god, Ahura Mazda, created twin spirits – one choosing
truth and light, the other untruth and darkness. The result
is a continuing struggle between Ahura Mazda,
represented by *Spenta Mainyu*, or Ahura Mazda's creative
energy, and Ahriman or *Angra Mainyu*, the destructive
spirit of darkness. Ultimately, Ahura Mazda will prevail
and time will end with all creation reuniting in Ahura
Mazda. The dualism of Zoroastrianism, embodied in such
opposites as life and death or light and dark or good and
evil, influenced the concept of the devil and of heaven
and hell in Christianity and the other Abrahamic
religions. For more than a millennium, until it was
displaced by Islam, Zoroastrianism was Persia's national
religion. In Zoroastrian cosmology fire is a symbol of
purity, hence the presence of lighted fires during prayer
rituals and the false idea that Zoroastrians worship fire.
Today there are probably fewer than 200,000
Zoroastrians in the world, with India's Parsees –
numbering around 70,000 – being the biggest group.
However, since the Parsees have a low birth rate and do
not seek converts, Zoroastrianism, the world's oldest
revealed religion after Judaism, is now one of its smallest.

List of isms

Abolitionism
Absenteeism
Absolutism
Abstract expressionism
Absurdism
Aestheticism
Afrocentrism
Ageism
Agnosticism
Agrarianism
Alarmism
Albigensianism
Albinism
Alcoholism
Altruism
American exceptionalism
Anabaptism
Anarchism
Anarcho-syndicalism
Aneurism
Anglicanism
Animism
Antagonism
Anthropocentrism
Anthropomorphism
Anthroposophism
Anti-Americanism

Anti-capitalism
Anti-communism
Antidisestablishmentarianism
Anti-fascism
Anti-globalism
Anti-imperialism
Antinomianism
Anti-Semitism
Aphorism
Arianism
Aristotelianism
Arminianism
Asceticism
Atavism
Atheism
Atomism
Authoritariansim
Autism
Ba'athism
Babism
Baha'ism
Balkanism
Baptism
Behaviouralism
Behaviourism
Bicameralism
Bilateralism

Bimetallism
Black nationalism
Blairism
Bogomilism
Bohemianism
Bolshevism
Bonapartism
Botulism
Bruxism
Buddhism
Bushism
Butskellism
Calvinism
Cannibalism
Capitalism
Careerism
Catastrophism
Catechism
Catharism
Catholicism
Centralism
Charlatanism
Chartism
Chauvinism
Christianism
Chromaticism
Chromatism
Classicism
Cognitivism
Collectivism
Colonialism

Commercialism
Communalism
Communism
Communitarianism
Conformism
Confucianism
Congregationalism
Consequentialism
Conservatism
Constructivism
Consumerism
Corporatism
Cosmopolitanism
Creationism
Cubism
Cynicism
Dadaism
Darbyism
Darwinism
Decentralism
Deconstructionism
Defeatism
Deism
Deontologism
Despotism
Determinism
Dialectical materialism
Dimorphism
Dispensationalism
Divisionism
Dixiecratism

Dogmatism
Donatism
Dualism
Dwarfism
Dystopianism
Eclecticism
Economism
Egalitarianism
Egocentrism
Egoism
Egotism
Elitism
Emotionalism
Empiricism
Environmentalism
Epicureanism
Episcopalianism
Essenism
Essentialism
Ethnocentrism
Euphemism
Euphuism
Eurocommunism
Evangelicalism
Evangelism
Exhibitionism
Existentialism
Exorcism
Expansionism
Expressionism
Extremism

Fabianism
Factionalism
Falangism
Fanaticism
Fascism
Fatalism
Fauvism
Favouritism
Federalism
Feminism
Fenianism
Fetishism
Feudalism
Fordism
Formalism
Fourierism
Francoism
Freudianism
Frotteurism
Fundamentalism
Futurism
Gallicanism
Gallicism
Gaullism
Geocentrism
Geophagism
Germanism
Gigantism
Globalism
Gnosticism
Goldwynism

Gradualism
Hasidism
Hedonism
Heightism
Heliocentrism
Hellenism
Henotheism
Hermaphroditism (or
   hermaphrodism)
Hermeticism
Heroism
Hinduism
Historical materialism
Historicism
Holism
Hooliganism
Humanism
Humanitarianism
Hypnotism
Hypopituitarism
Idealism
Ignosticism
Imagism
Imperialism
Impressionism
Individualism
Intellectualism
Intentionalism
Internationalism
Interpretivism
Interventionism

Irredentism
Islamism
Isolationism
Isomorphism
Jacksonianism
Jacobinism
Jainism
Jansenism
Jihadism
Jingoism
Journalism
Judaism
Kabbalism
Keynesianism
Know-nothingism
Lacanianism
Lamarckism
Latitudinarianism
Leftism
Legalism
Leninism
Lesbianism
Liberalism
Libertarianism
Libertinism
Literalism
Localism
Logical positivism
Lollardism
Luddism (also Ludditism)
Luminism

Lutheranism
Lyricism
Lysenkoism
Machiavellianism
Malapropism
Malthusianism
Manichaeism
Mannerism
Maoism
Marxism
Marxism-Leninism
Masochism
Materialism
Mazdaism
McCarthyism
Mechanism
Meliorism
Menshevism
Mercantilism
Mesmerism
Metabolism
Methodism
Militarism
Millenarianism
Millennialism
Minimalism
Mithraism
Modernism
Monarchism
Monasticism
Monetarism

Monism
Monophysitism
Monopolism
Monotheism
Monotheletism (or
    monothelitism)
Montanism
Moral absolutism
Moralism
Moral objectivism
Moral relativism
Moral universalism
Mormonism
Muggletonianism
Multiculturalism
Multilateralism
Mutualism
Mysticism
Narcissism
Nationalism
National Socialism
Naturalism
Naturism
Nazism
Neocatastrophism
Neoclassicism
Neoconservatism
Neo-Darwinism
Neo-interventionism
Neoliberalism
Neologism

Neoplasticism
Neoplatonism
Nepotism
Nestorianism
Nihilism
Nominalism
Nonconformism
Non-interventionism
Nudism
Objectivism
Obscurantism
Occasionalism
Oligopolism
Onanism
Optimism
Organism
Orientalism
Orphism
Ostracism
Pacifism
Paganism
Paleoconservatism
Pan-Africanism
Pan-Arabism
Panentheism
Pan-Germanism
Pan-Slavism
Pantheism
Parallelism
Parasitism
Pastafarianism

Pastoralism
Paternalism
Patriotism
Pauperism
Pelagianism
Pentecostalism
Perfectionism
Peronism
Pessimism
Phalangism
Phallocentrism
Pharisaism
Phenomenalism
Photojournalism
Pietism
Plagiarism
Platonism
Pluralism
Plutonism
Pointillism
Polymorphism
Polytheism
Populism
Positivism
Postcolonialism
Postmodernism
Poststructuralism
Pragmatism
Presbyterianism
Presentism
Priapism

Prism
Progressivism
Proselytism
Protectionism
Protestantism
Puritanism
Quakerism
Quietism
Quixotism
Racialism
Racism
Radicalism
Randianism
Rastafarianism
Rationalism
Reaganism
Realism
Reductionism
Regalism
Regionalism
Relativism
Republicanism
Revisionism
Rightism
Roman Catholicism
Romanticism
Rosicrucianism
Sabbatarianism
Sacerdotalism
Sadism
Salafism

Sapphism
Satanism
Scandinavism
Schism
Scholasticism
Scientism
Sectarianism
Secularism
Sensationalism
Sensualism
Separatism
Serialism
Sexism
Shamanism
Shiism
Shintoism
Sikhism
Social Darwinism
Socialism
Solecism
Solipsism
Sophism
Spiritualism
Spoonerism
Stalinism
Statism
Stoicism
Structuralism
Sufism
Surrealism
Syllogism

Symbolism
Syndicalism
Tantrism
Taoism
Taylorism
Terrorism
Thatcherism
Theism
Totalitarianism
Totemism
Transcendentalism
Transvestism (or
    transvesticism)
Triumphalism
Tropism
Trotskyism
Ultramontanism
Uniformitarianism
Unilateralism
Unionism

Unitarianism
Universalism
Utilitarianism
Utopianism
Valetudinarianism
Vandalism
Veganism
Vegetarianism
Vorticism
Voyeurism
Vulgarism
Wahhabism
Whiggism
White nationalism
Witticism
Zeism
Zionism
Zoomorphism
Zoroastrianism